Ages 3+

Pre-K Skills Series

READY FOR

Preschool

Dot Markers Activity Book

400+ Pages of FUN

Letters & Numbers

Pre-K Skills Series Book 1 — Letters & Numbers — READY FOR Preschool Dot Markers Activity Book — With BIG DOT Circles

Pre-K Skills Series Book 2 — Lines & Shapes — READY FOR Preschool Dot Markers Activity Book — With BIG DOT Circles

Lines & Shapes

Sight Words

Pre-K Skills Series Book 3 — Sight Words — READY FOR Preschool Dot Markers Activity Book — With BIG DOT Circles

Pre-K Skills Series Book 4 — Numbers & Counting — READY FOR Preschool Dot Markers Activity Book — With BIG DOT Circles

Numbers & Counting

Ages 3+

Pre-K Skills Series Book 1
· · · · · · · · · ·
Letters & Numbers

READY FOR
Preschool
Dot Markers Activity Book

With BIG DOT Circles

worm

four

Find and dot FOUR circles.

Black reverse pages for less bleed-through!

airplane

bicycle

cat

dog

elephant

flower

giraffe

Hh

house

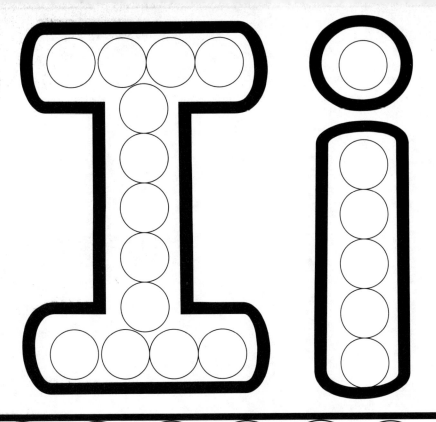

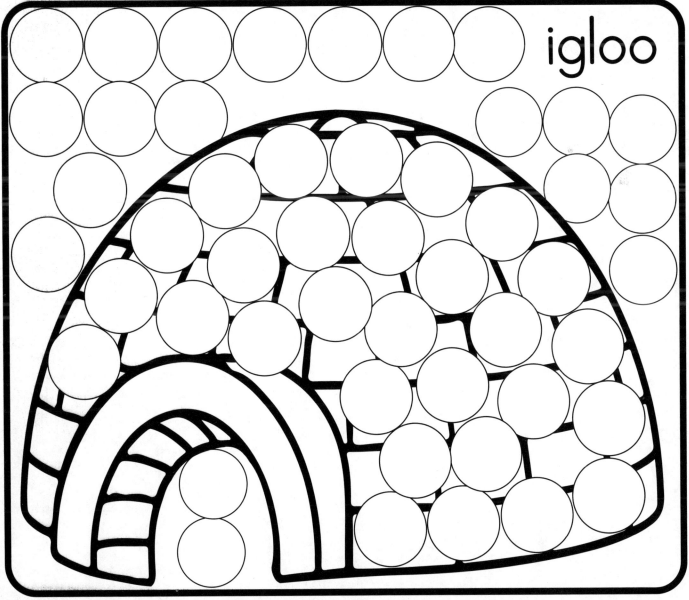

igloo

jellyfish

koala

lion

motorcycle

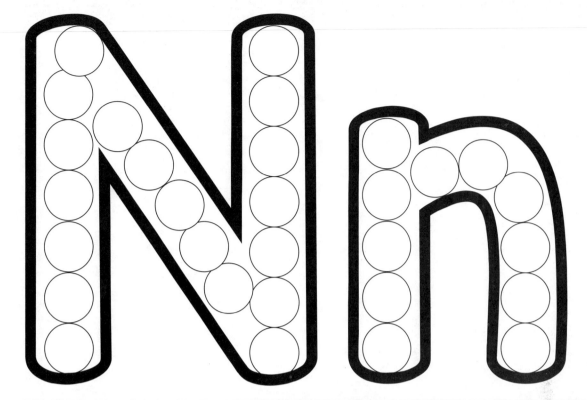

nest

otter

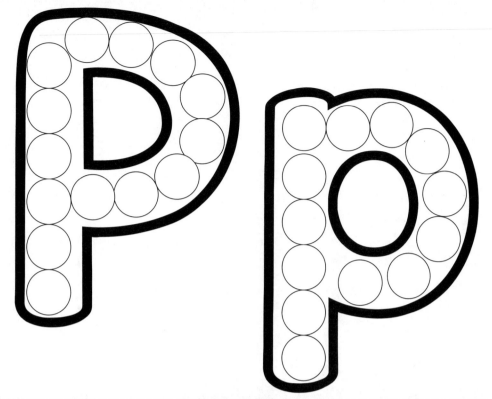

penguin

queen

rabbit

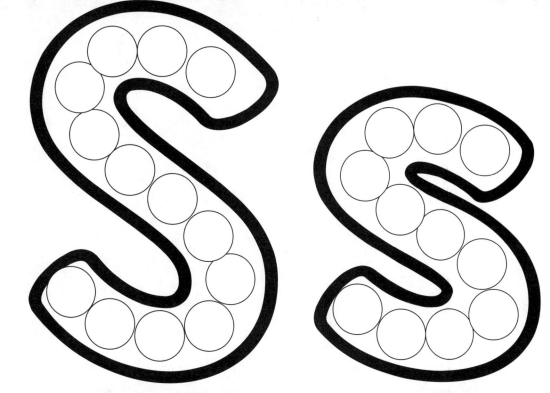

swordfish

train

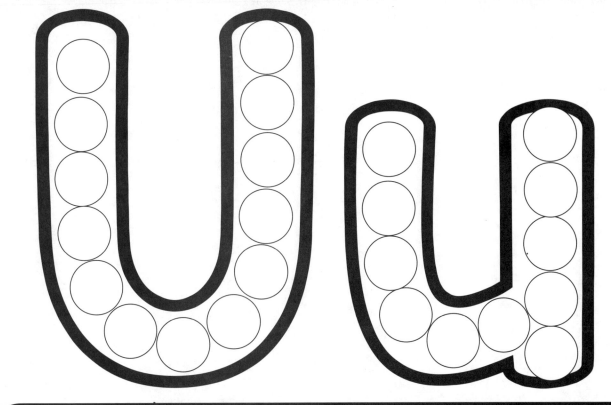

unicorn

volcano

worm

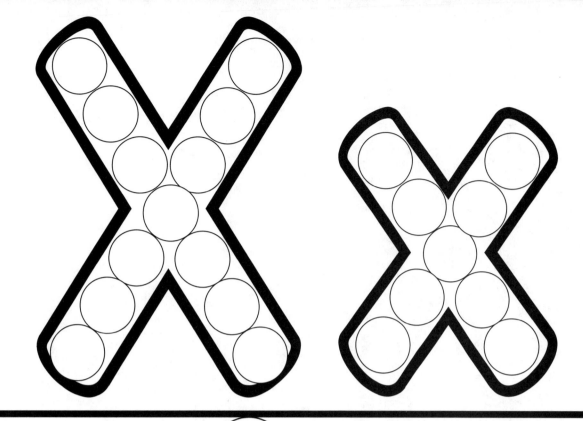

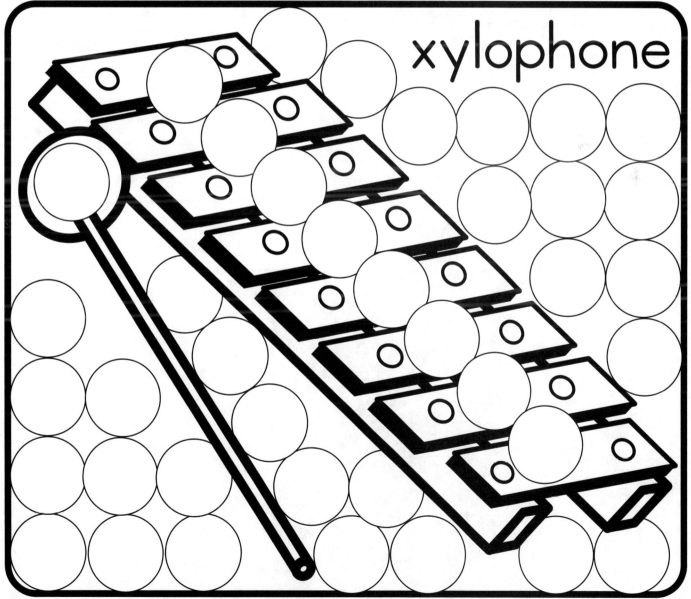

xylophone

yak

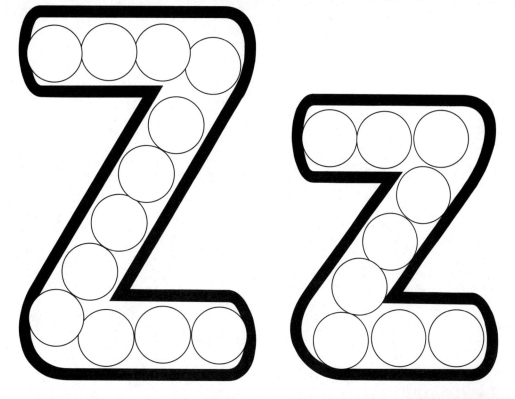

zebra

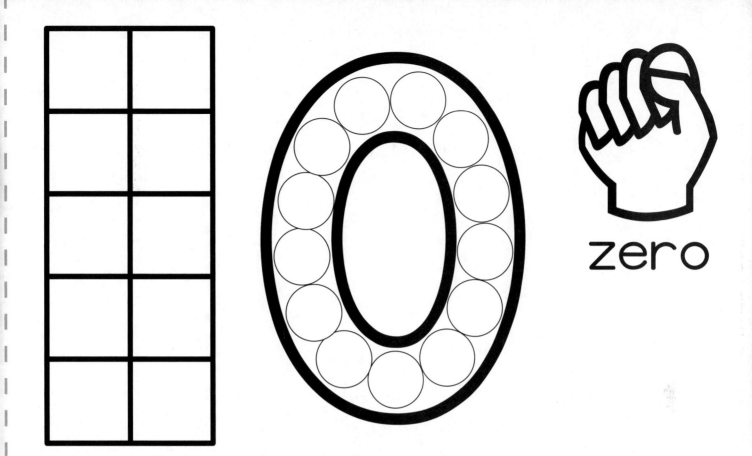

zero

Find and dot ZERO diamonds.

Hint: There are none!

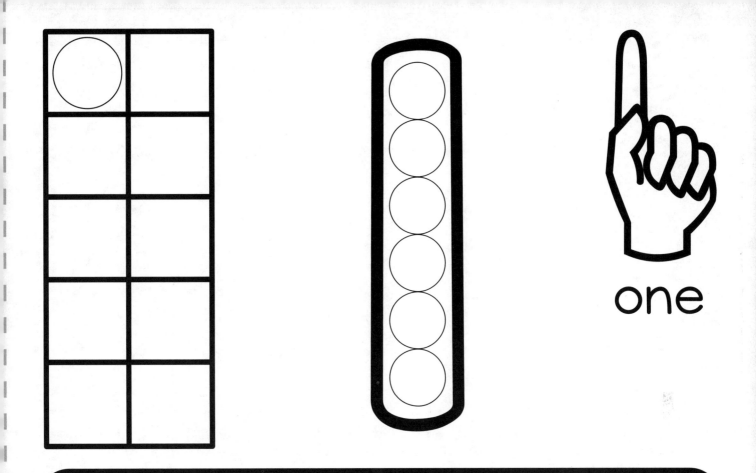

one

Find and dot ONE heart.

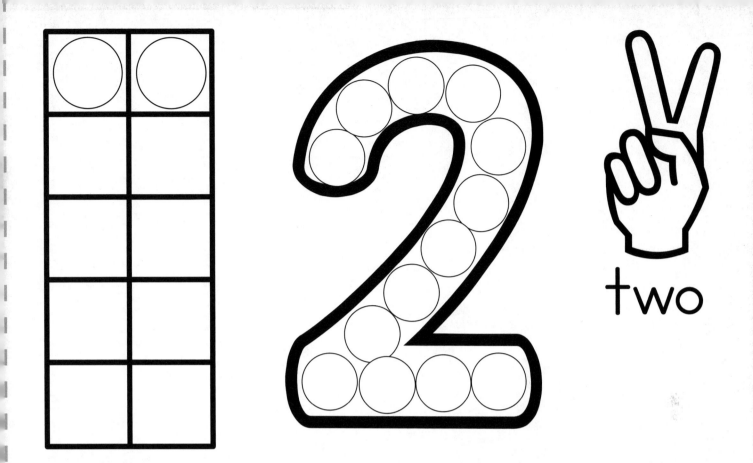

two

Find and dot TWO stars.

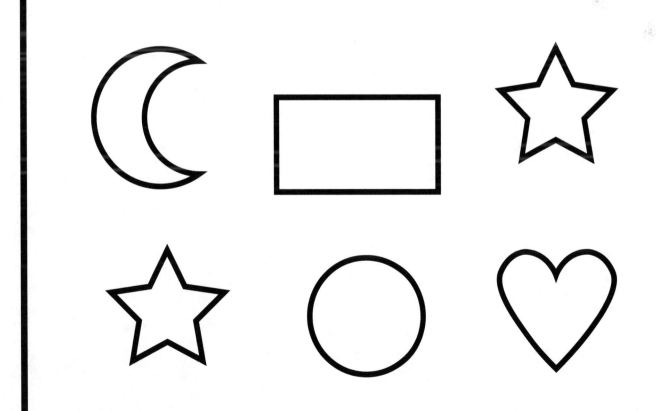

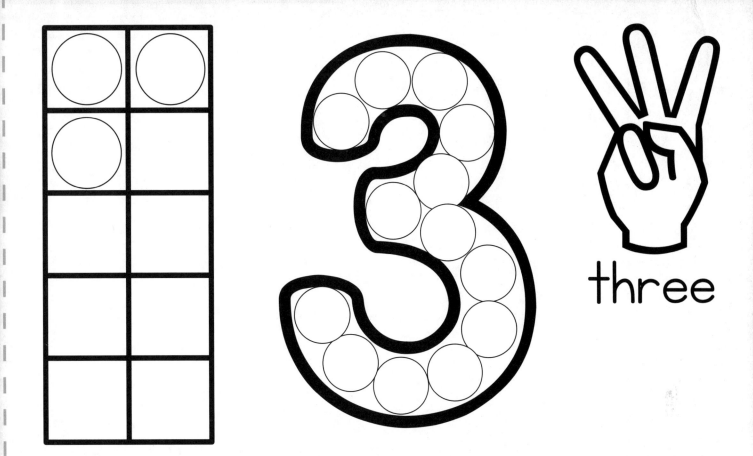

three

Find and dot THREE moons.

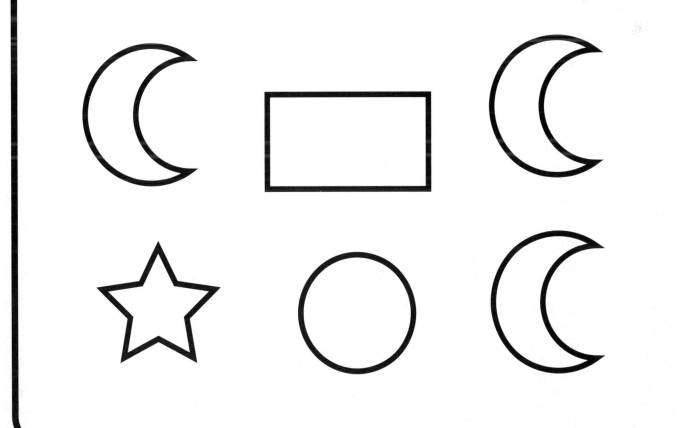

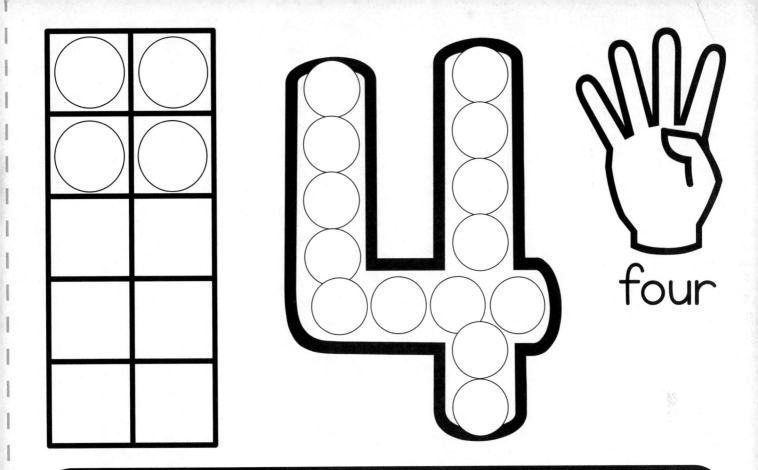

four

Find and dot FOUR circles.

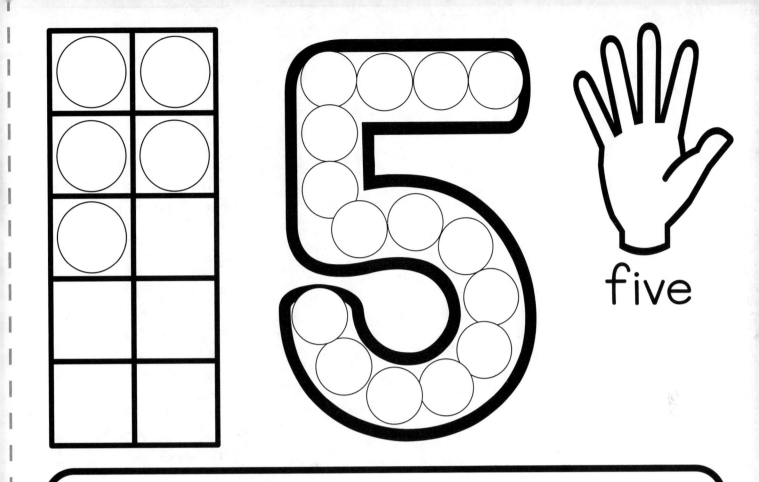

five

Find and dot FIVE squares.

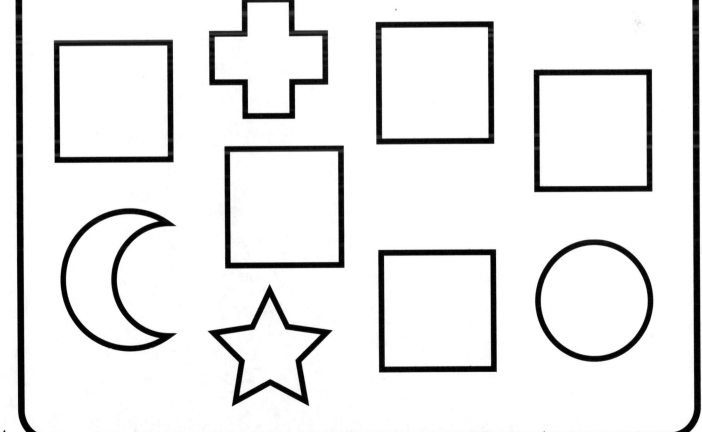

six

Find and dot SIX rectangles.

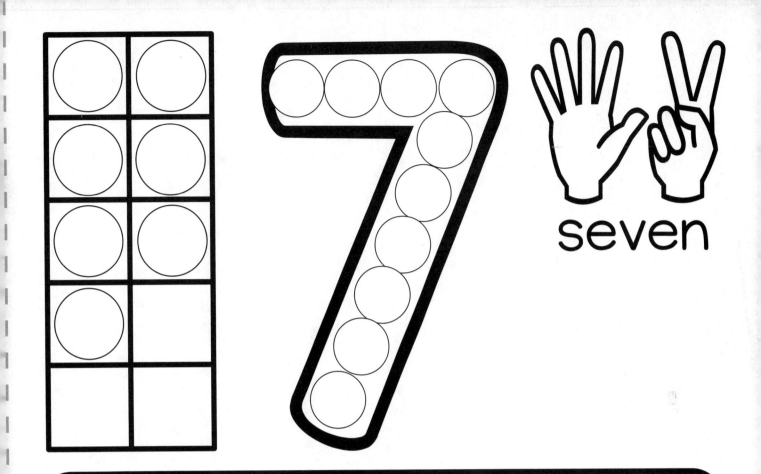

seven

Find and dot SEVEN ovals.

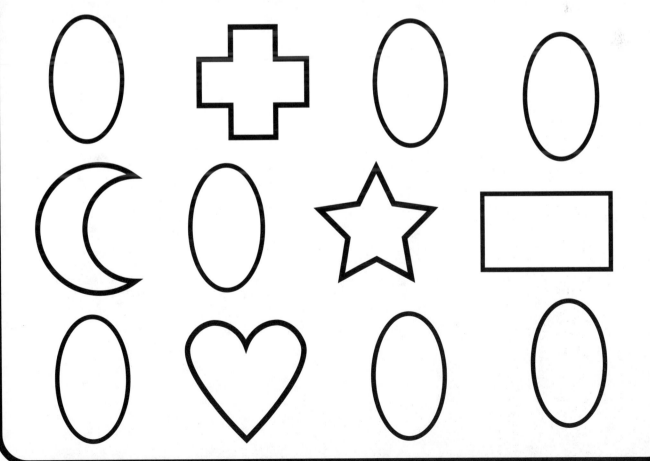

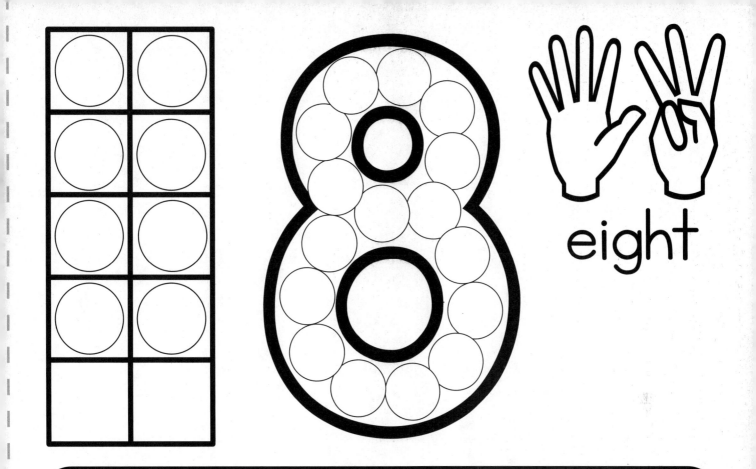

eight

Find and dot EIGHT pluses.

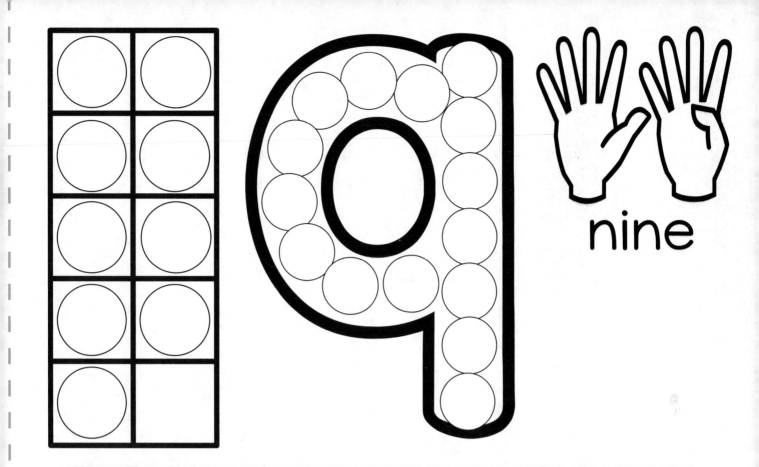

nine

Find and dot NINE triangles.

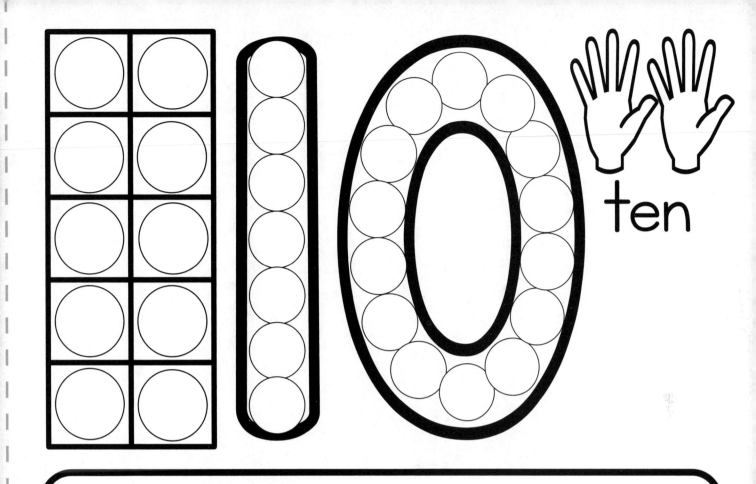

ten

Find and dot TEN pentagons.

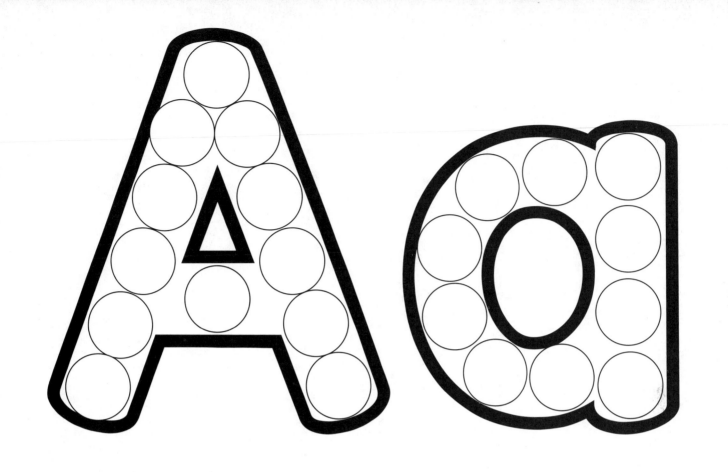
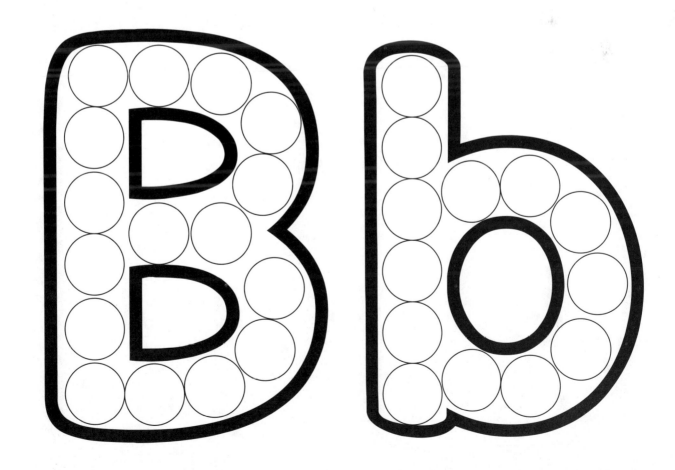

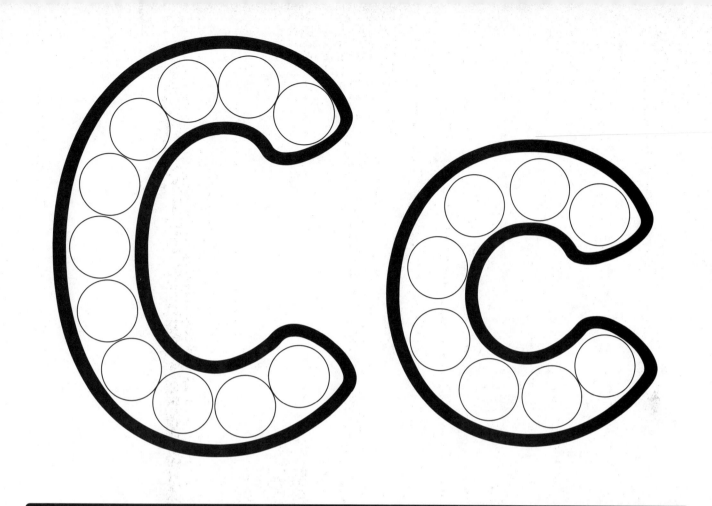

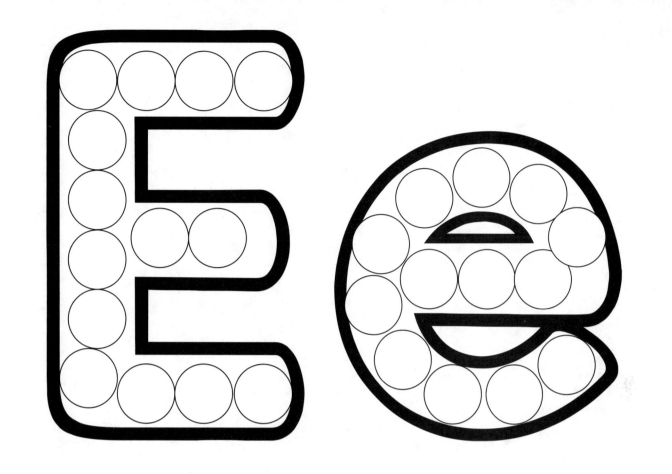

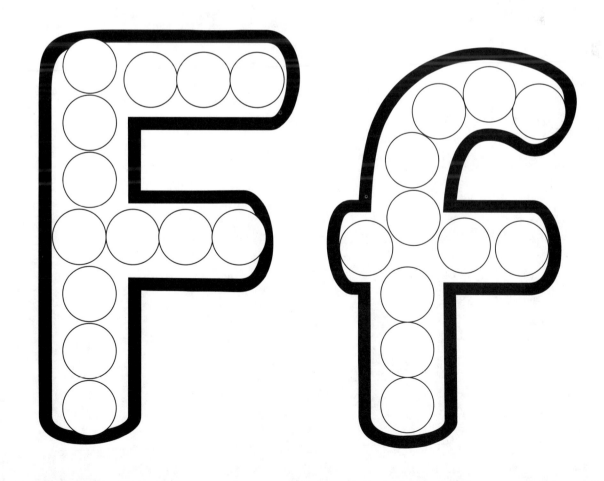

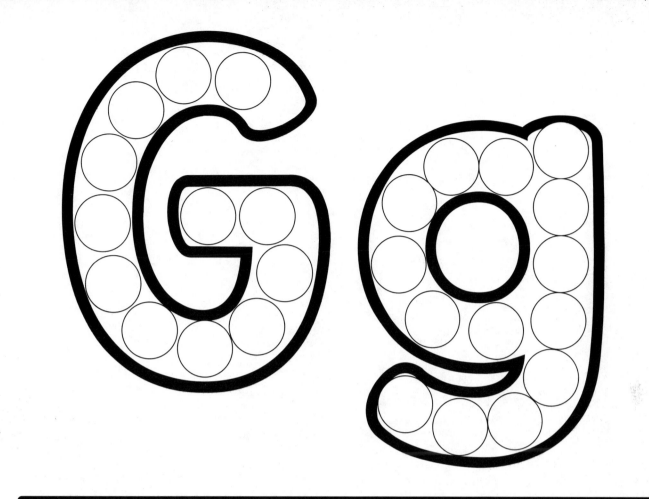

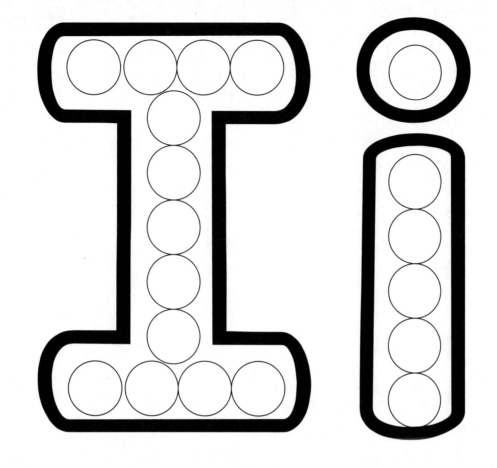

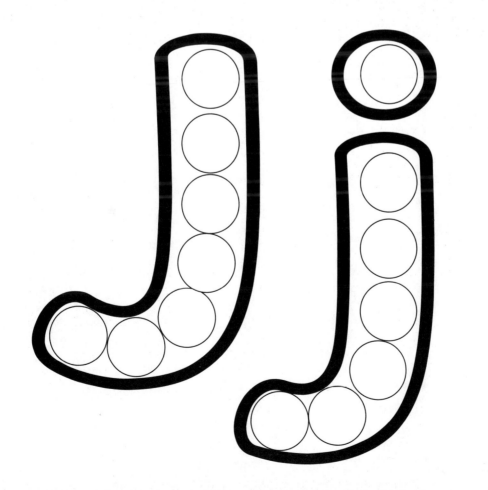

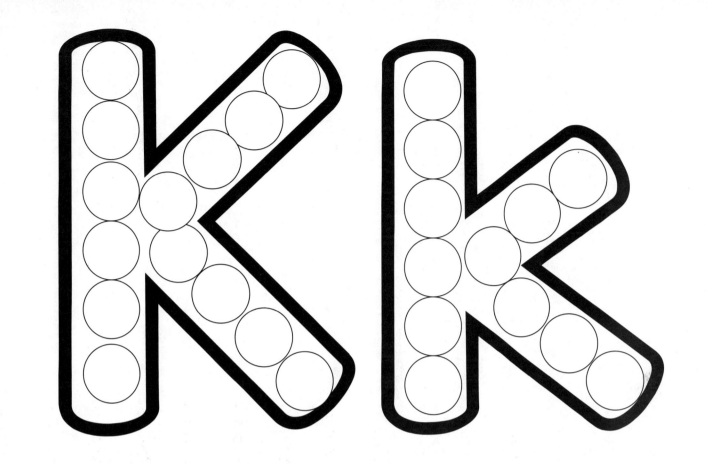

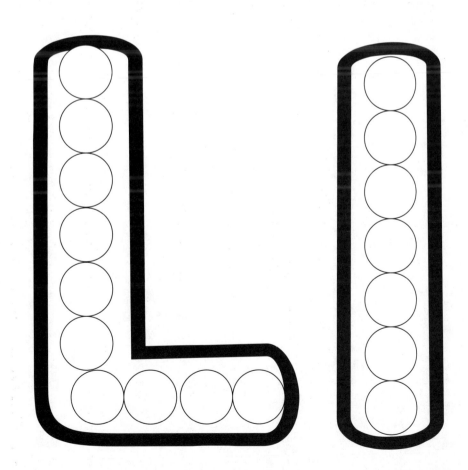

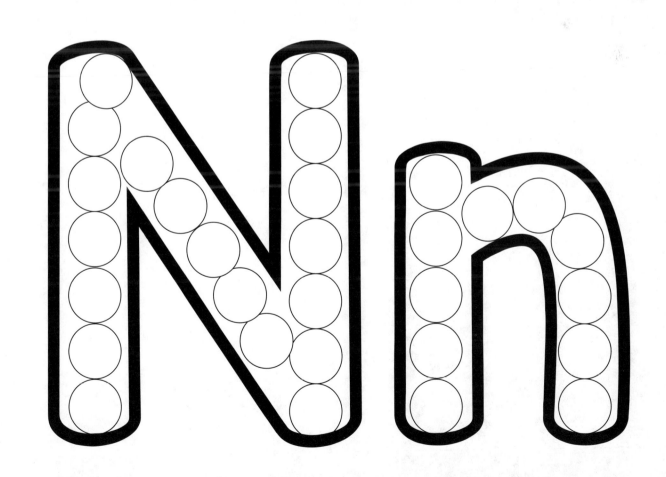

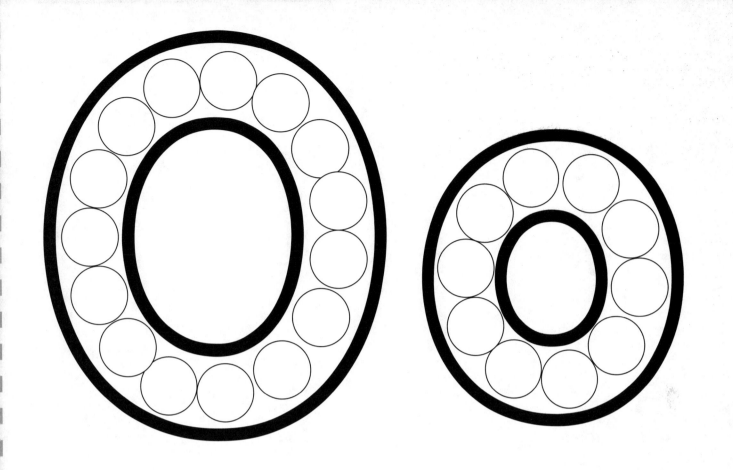

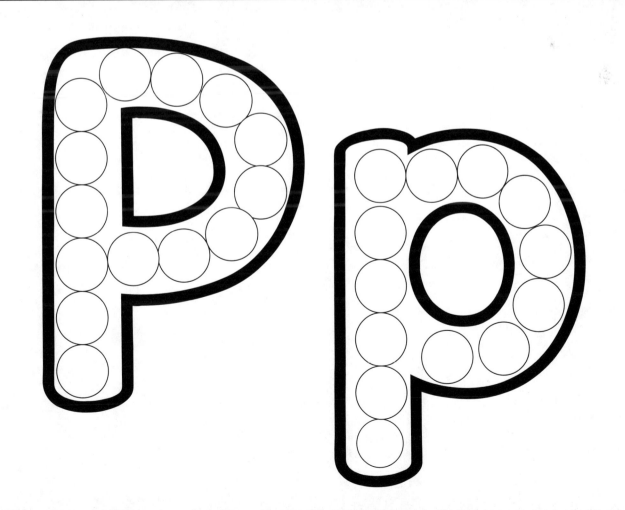

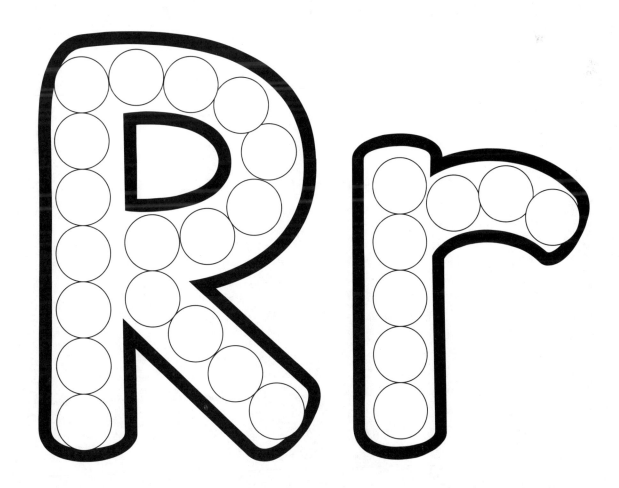

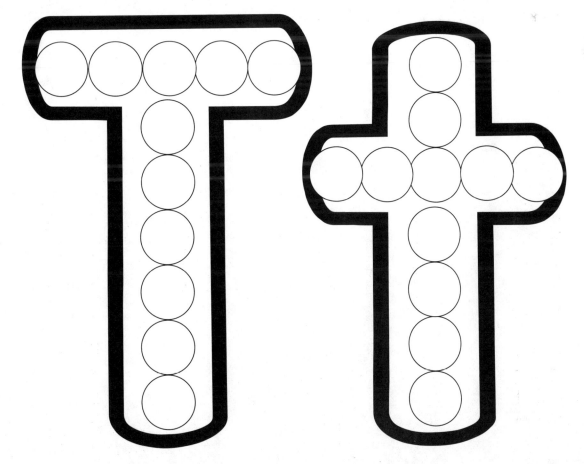

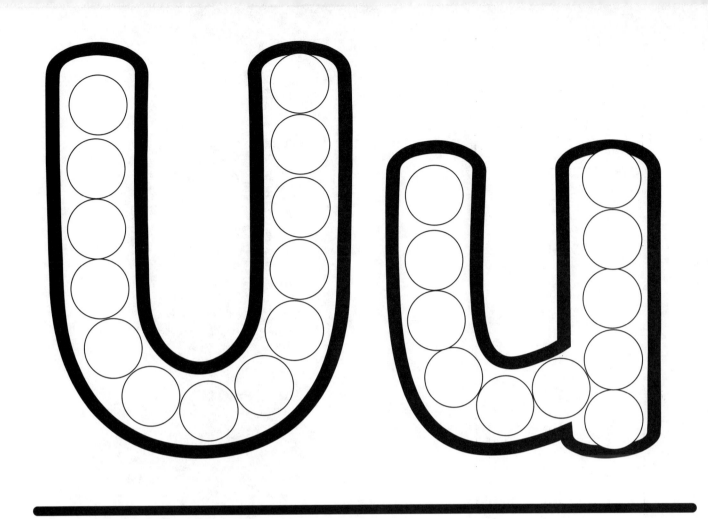

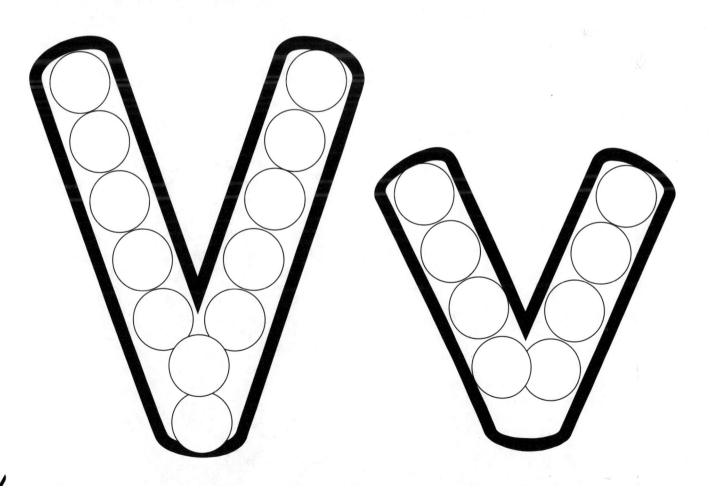

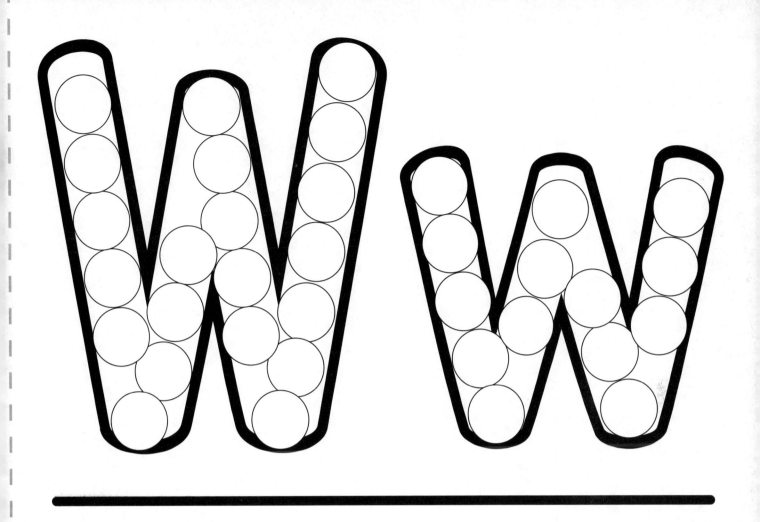

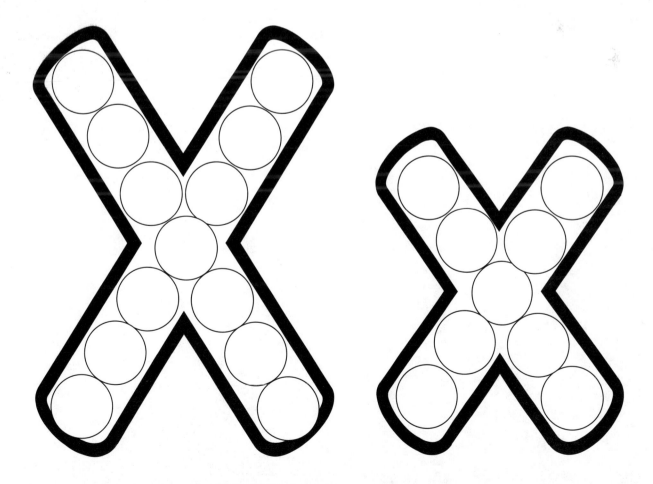

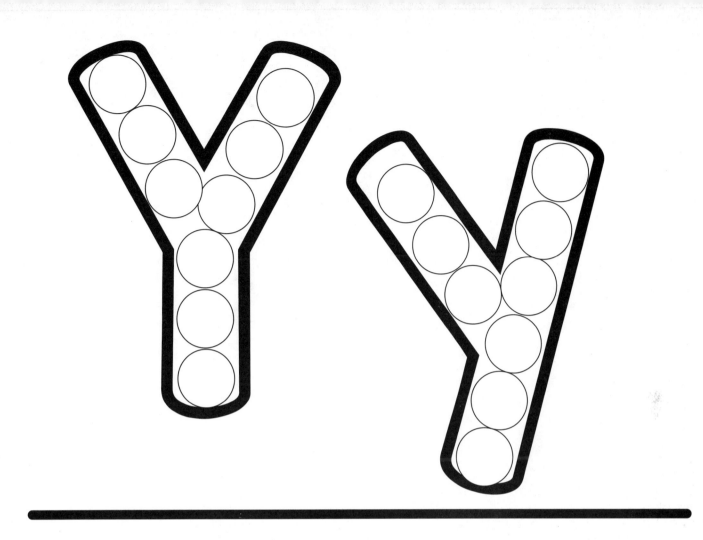
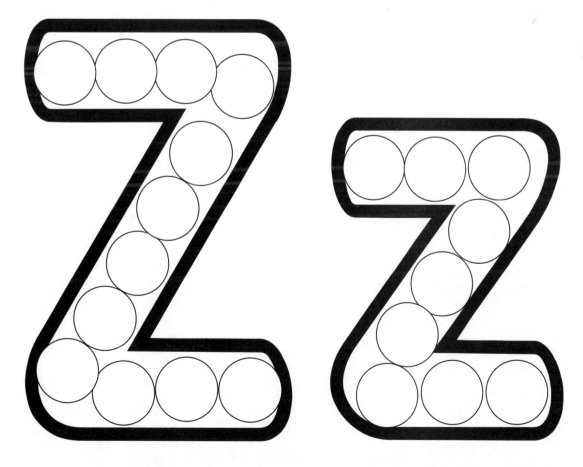

Ages 3+

Pre-K Skills Series Book 2

Lines & Shapes

READY FOR Preschool

Dot Markers Activity Book

With BIG DOT Circles

What's the shape?

Circle

Dot all the stars.

Dot the lines.

Black reverse pages for less bleed-through!

Dot the lines.

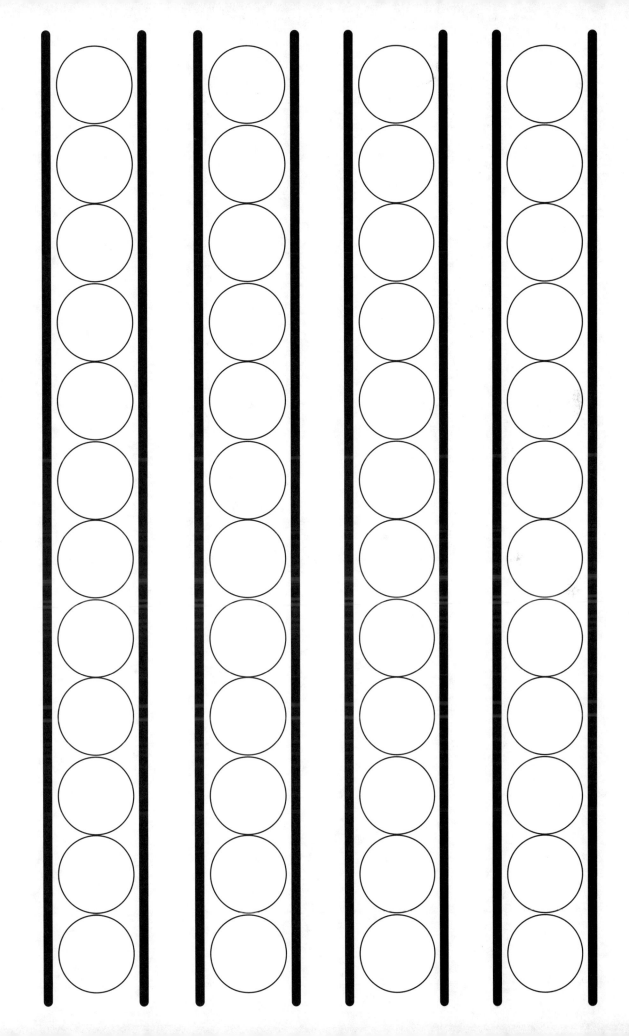

What's the shape?

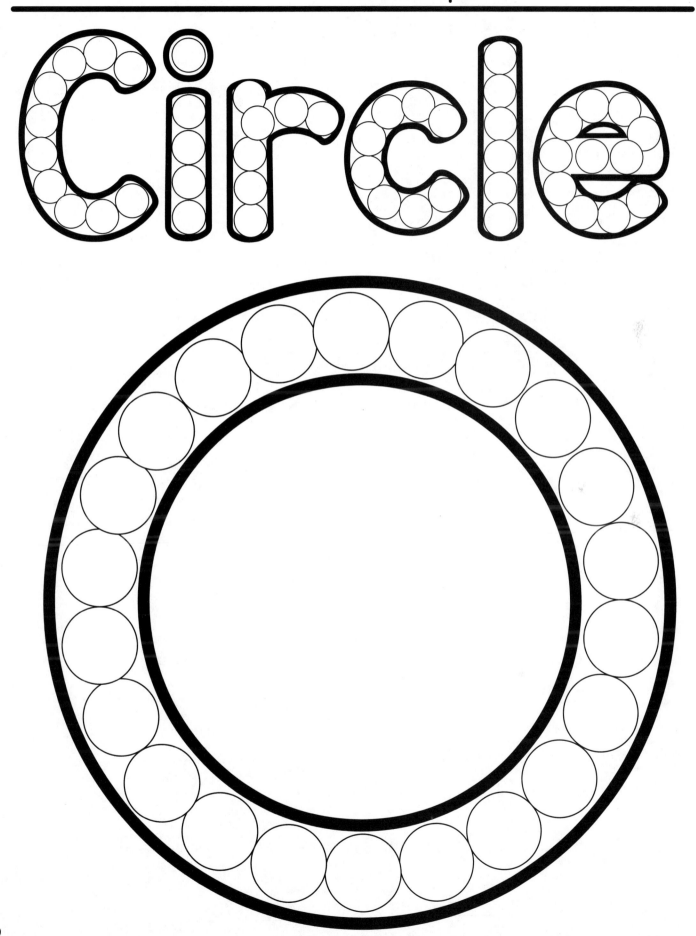

Circle

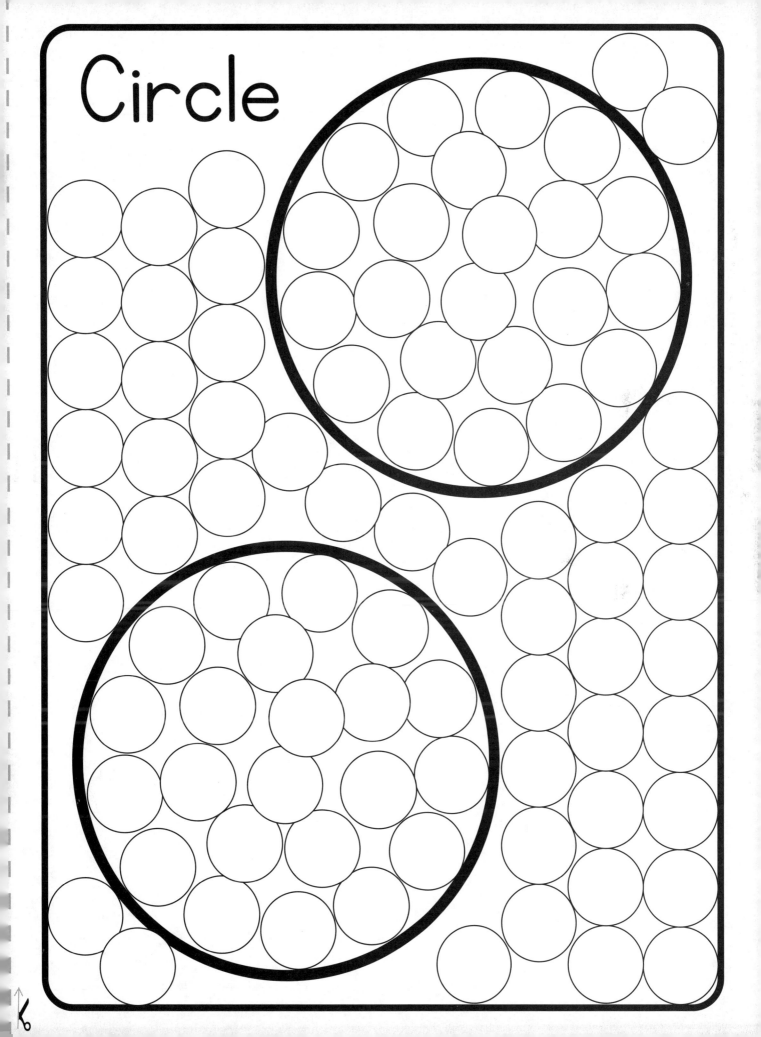

Dot all the circles.

Dot the lines.

What's the shape?

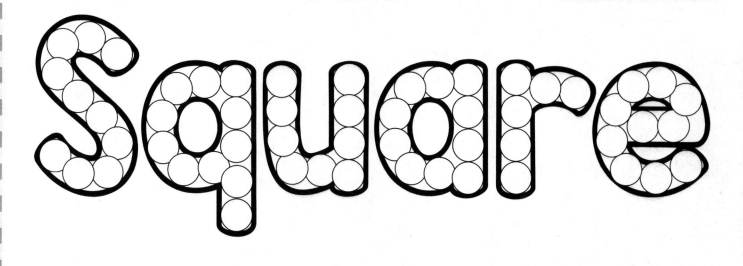

Square

Dot all the squares.

Dot the lines.

What's the shape?

Star

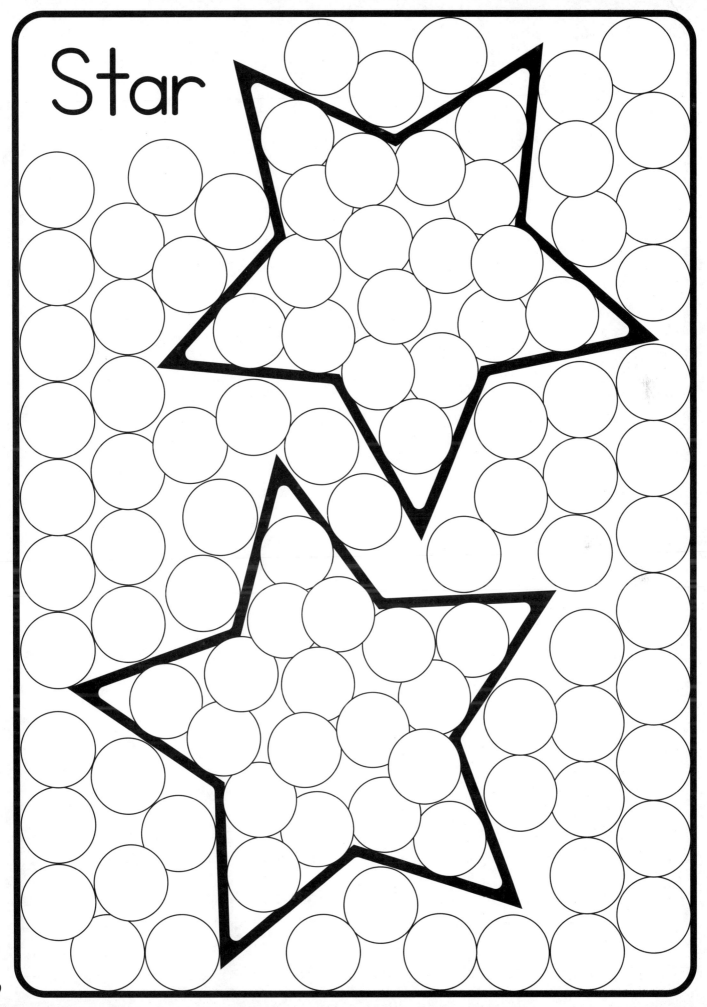

Dot all the stars.

Dot the lines.

What's the shape?

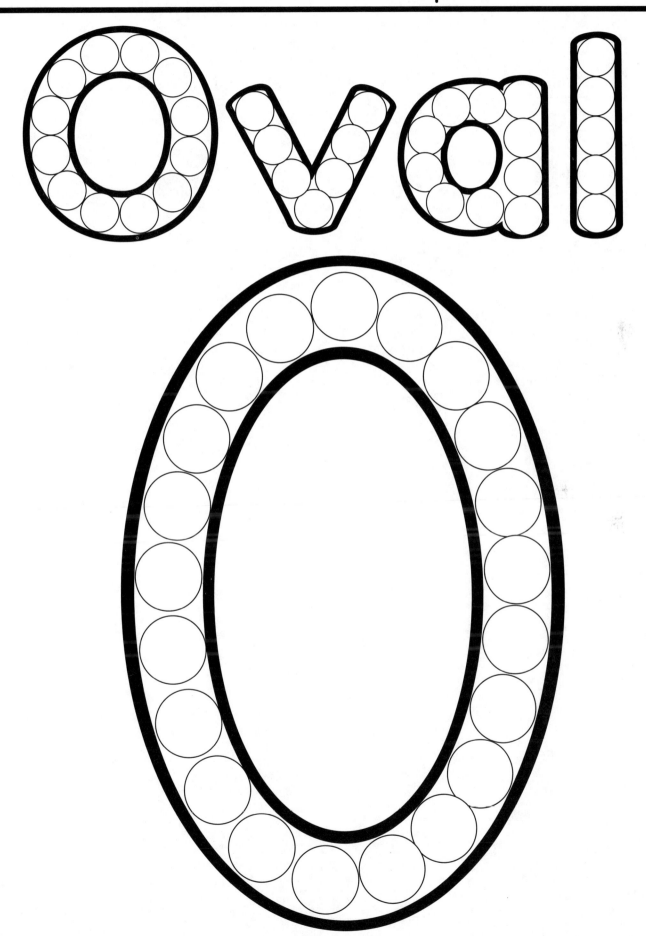

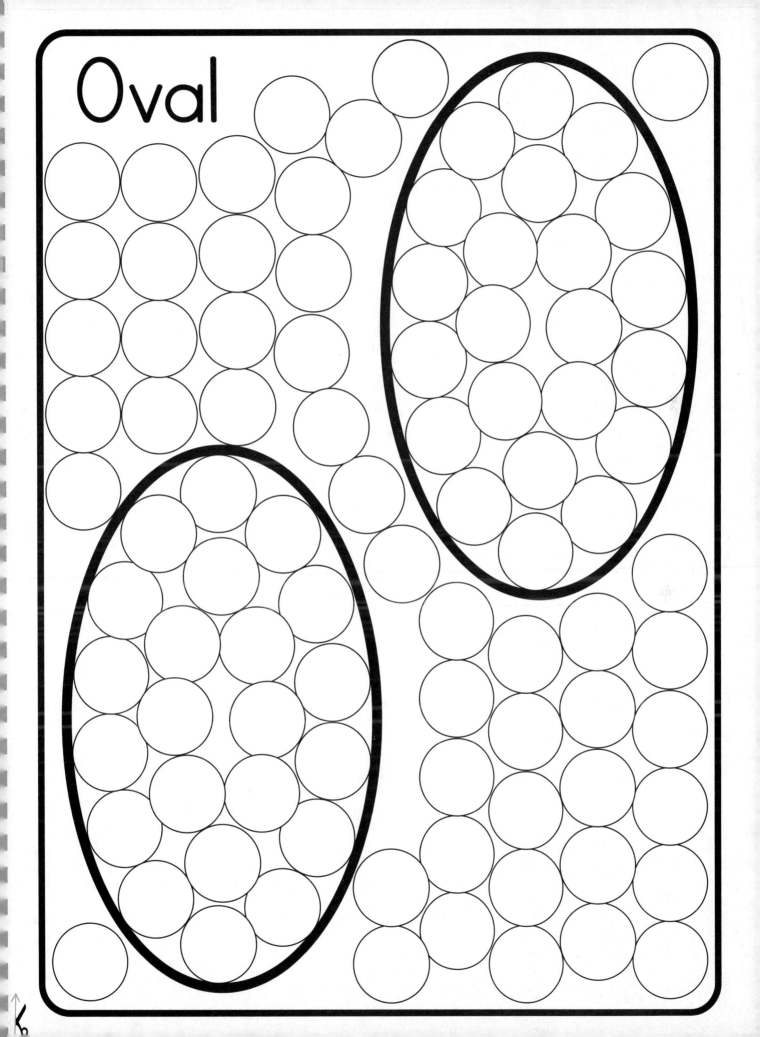

Oval

Dot all the ovals.

Dot the lines.

What's the shape?

Triangle

Triangle

Dot all the triangles.

Dot the lines.

What's the shape?

Heart

Dot all the hearts.

Dot the lines.

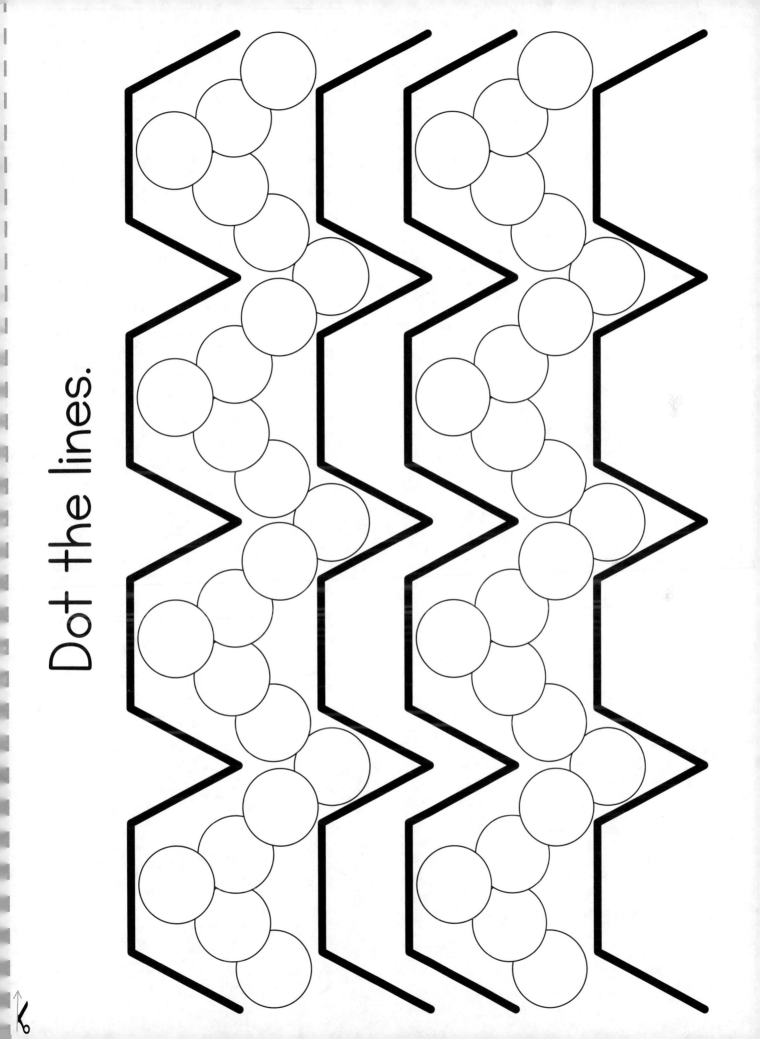

What's the shape?

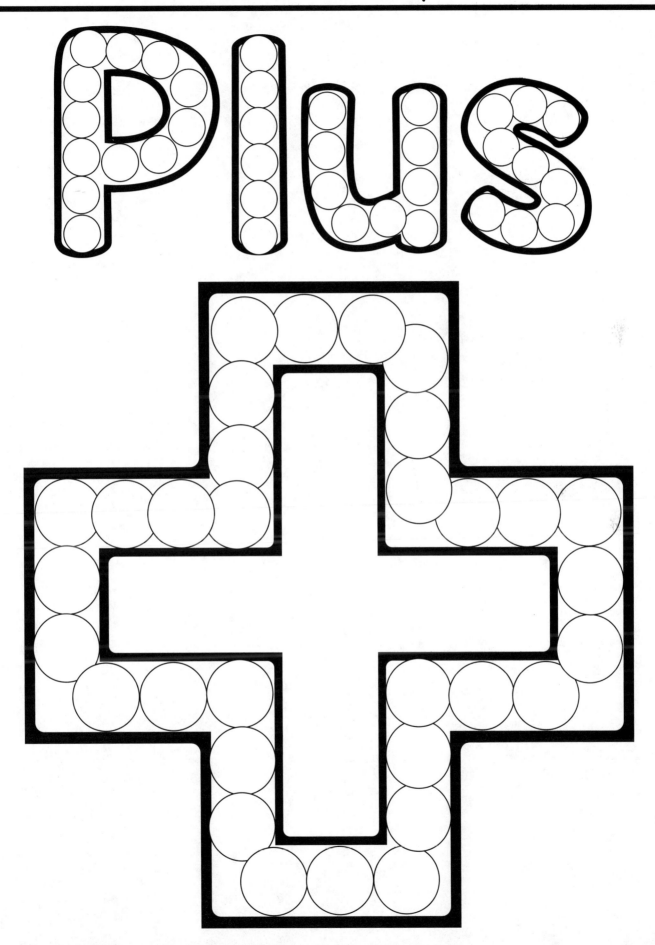

Plus Sign

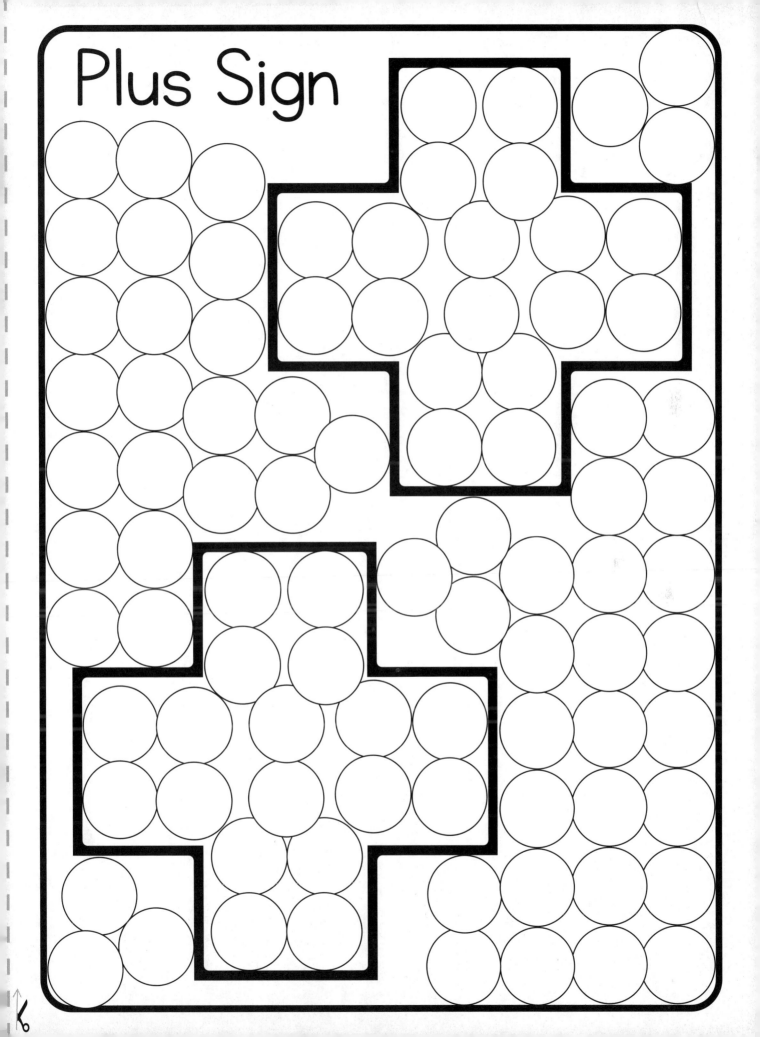

Dot all the plus signs.

Dot the lines.

What's the shape?

Dot all the moons.

Dot the lines.

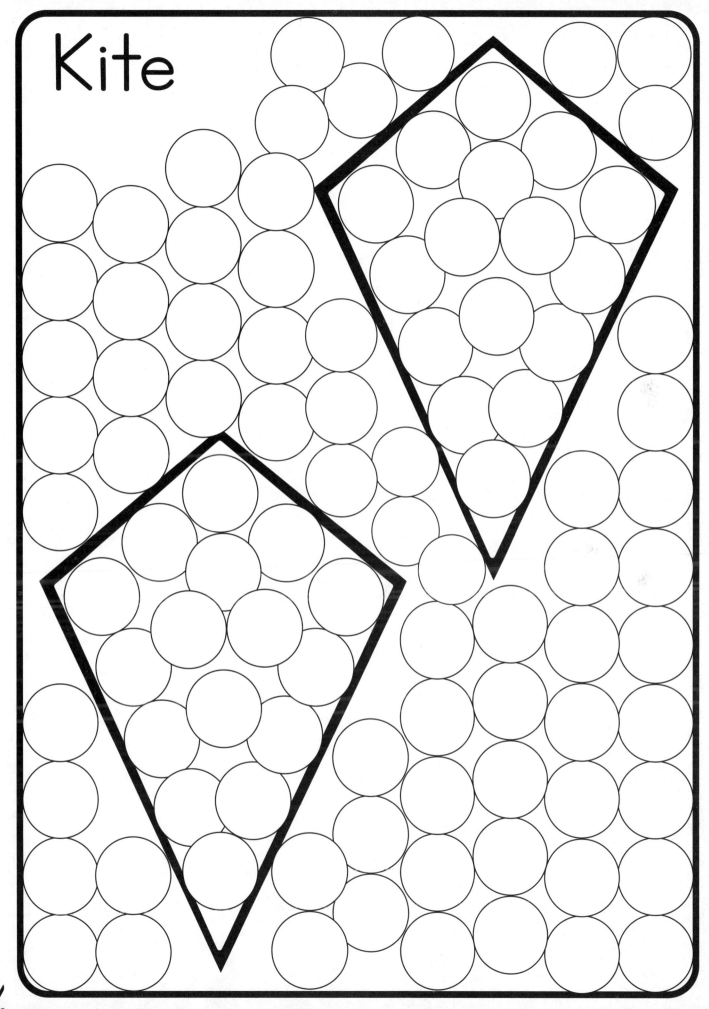

Kite

Dot all the kites.

Dot the lines.

What's the shape?

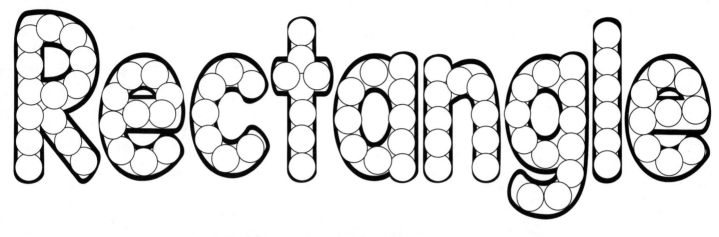

Rectangle

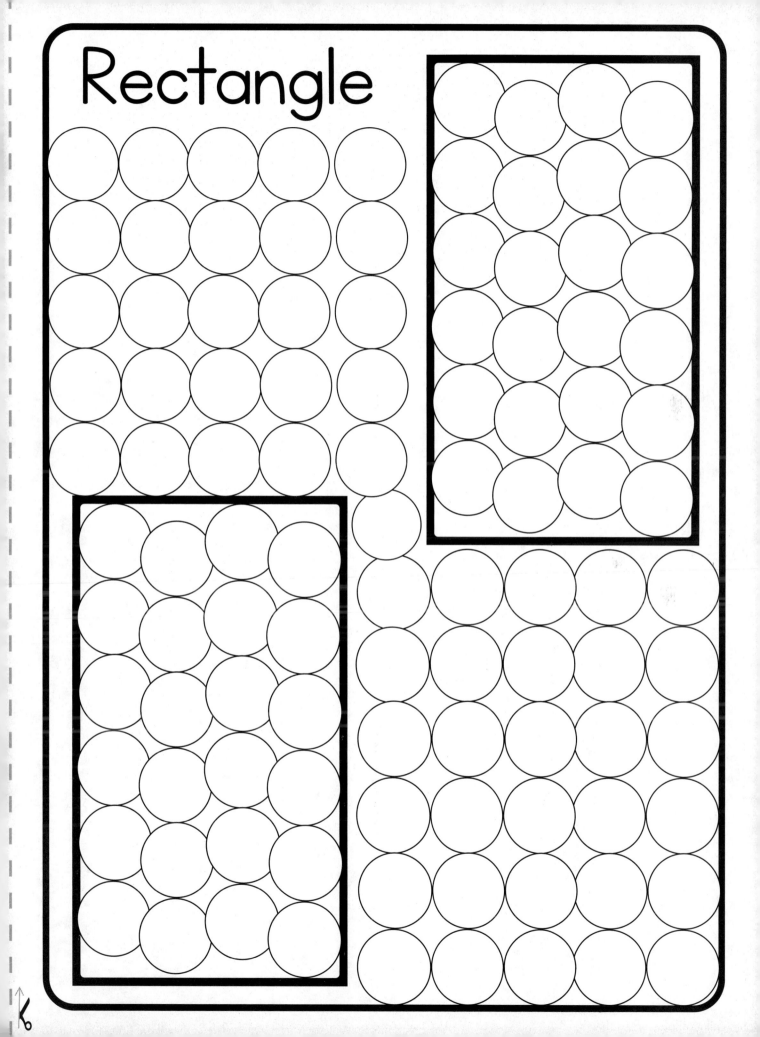

Dot all the rectangles.

Dot the lines.

What's the shape?

Diamond

Diamond

Dot all the diamonds.

Dot the lines.

What's the shape?

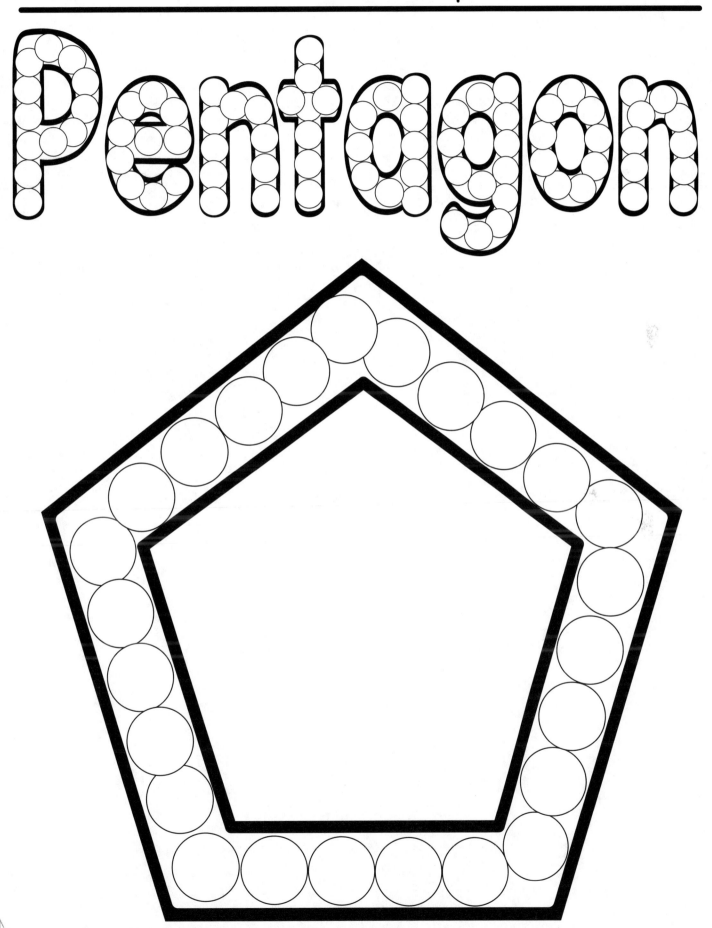

Pentagon

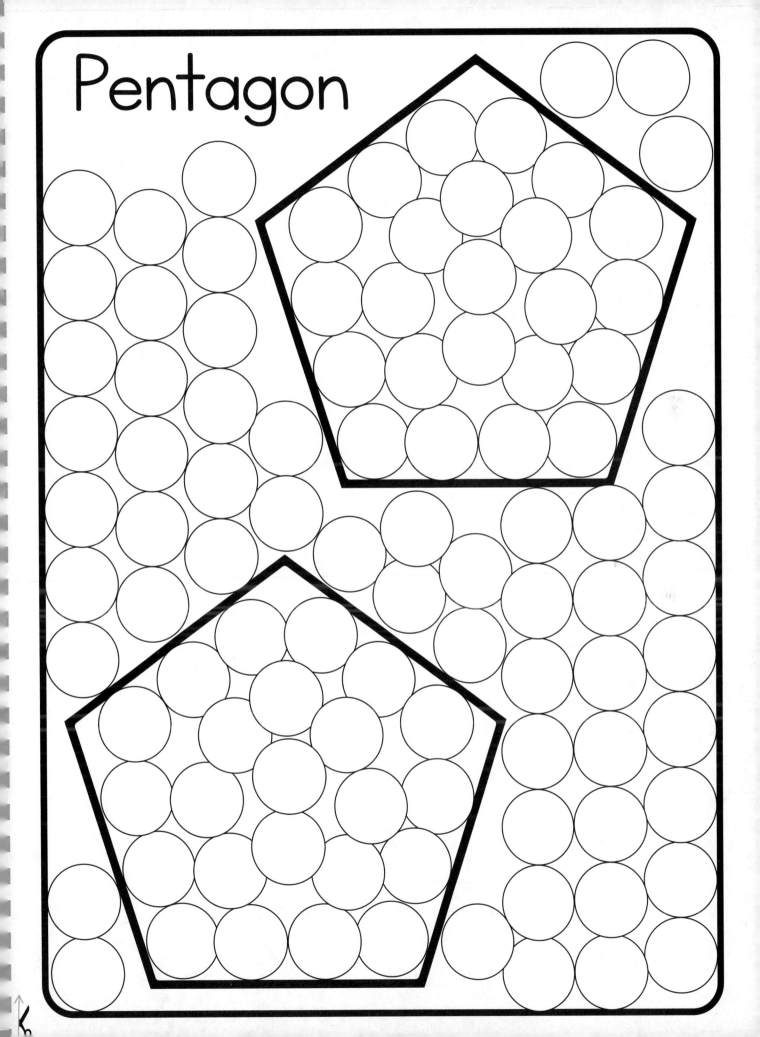

Dot all the pentagons.

Dot the lines.

What's the shape?

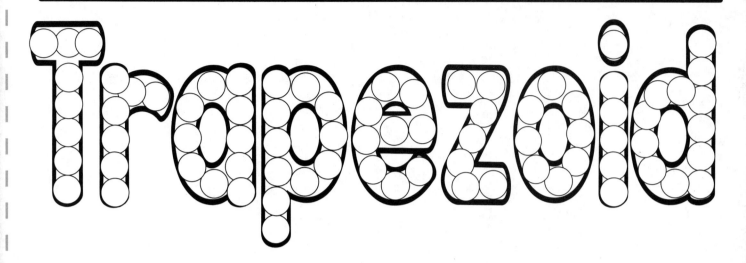

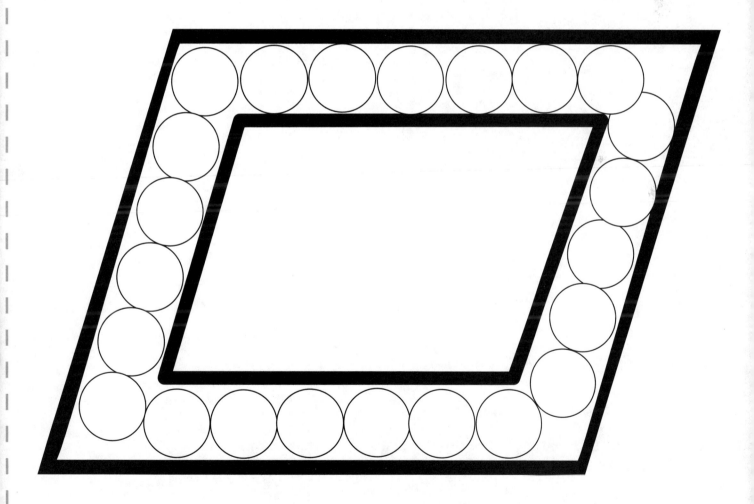

Trapezoid

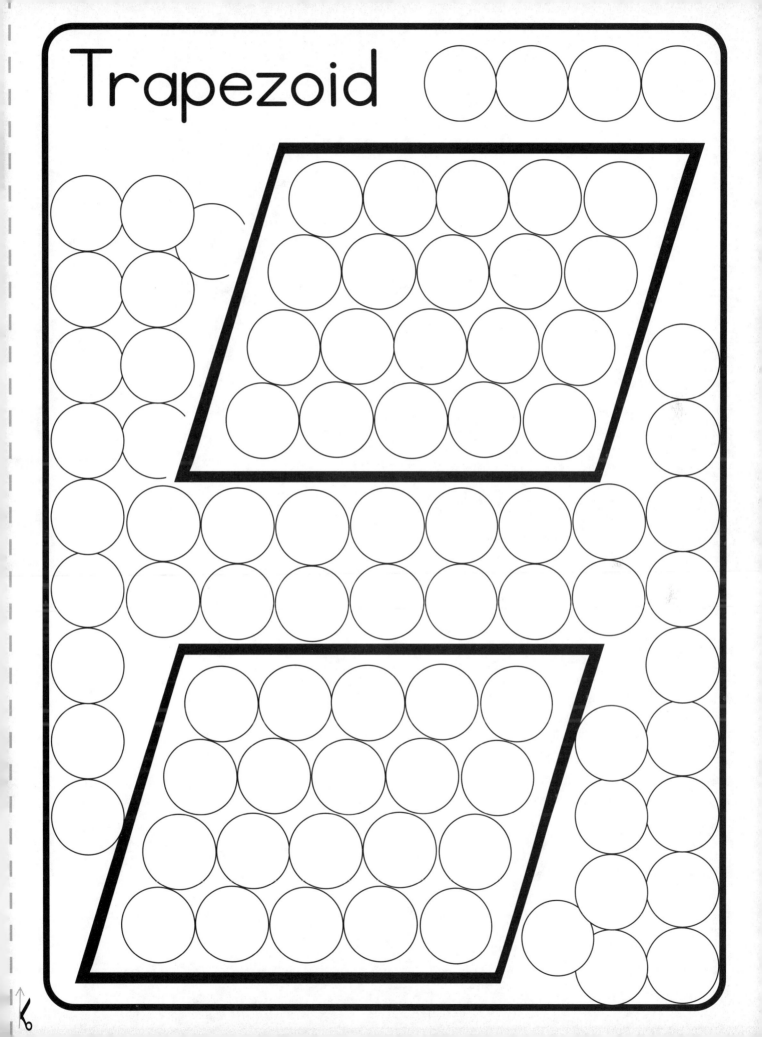

Dot all the trapezoids.

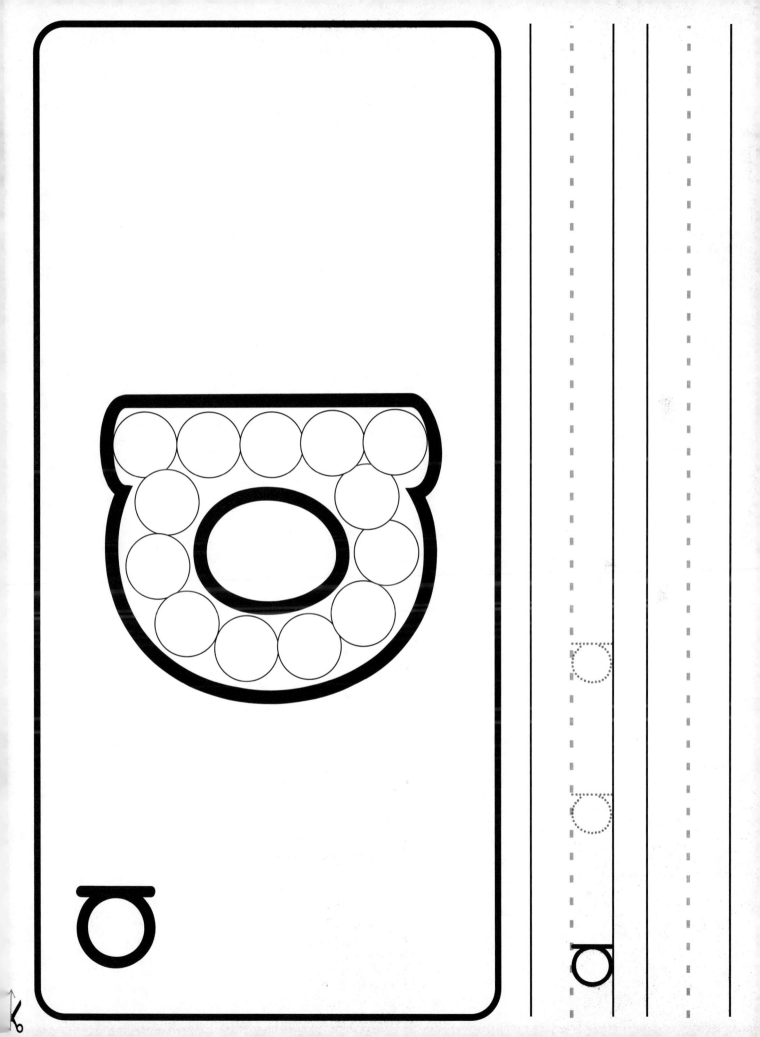

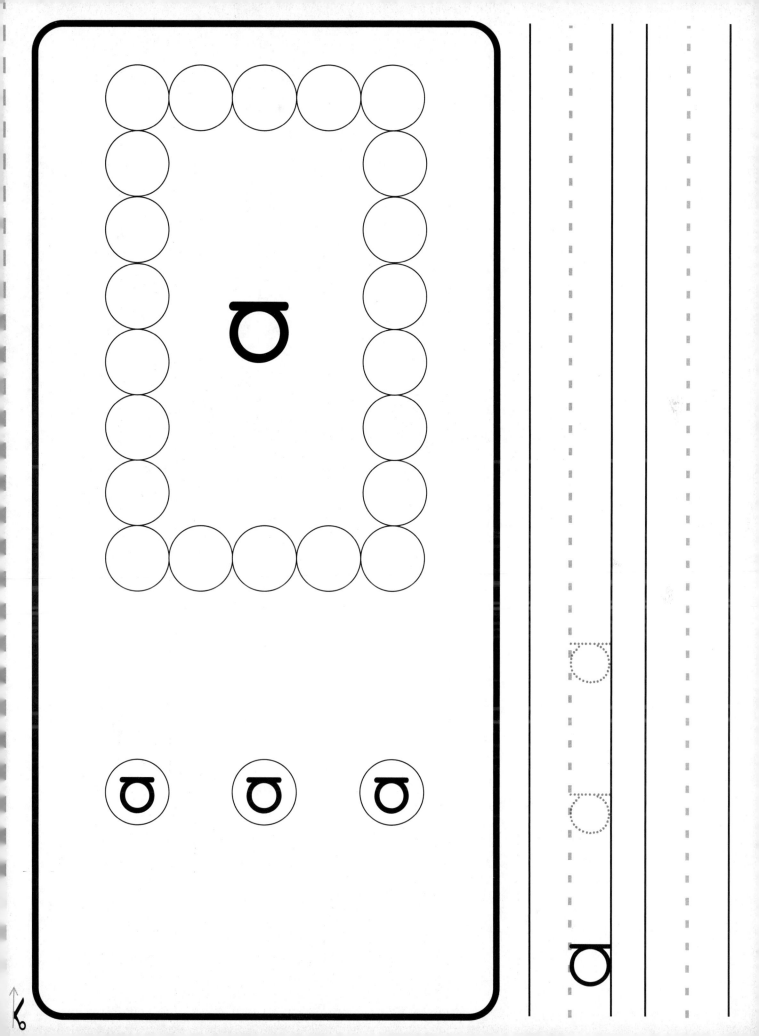

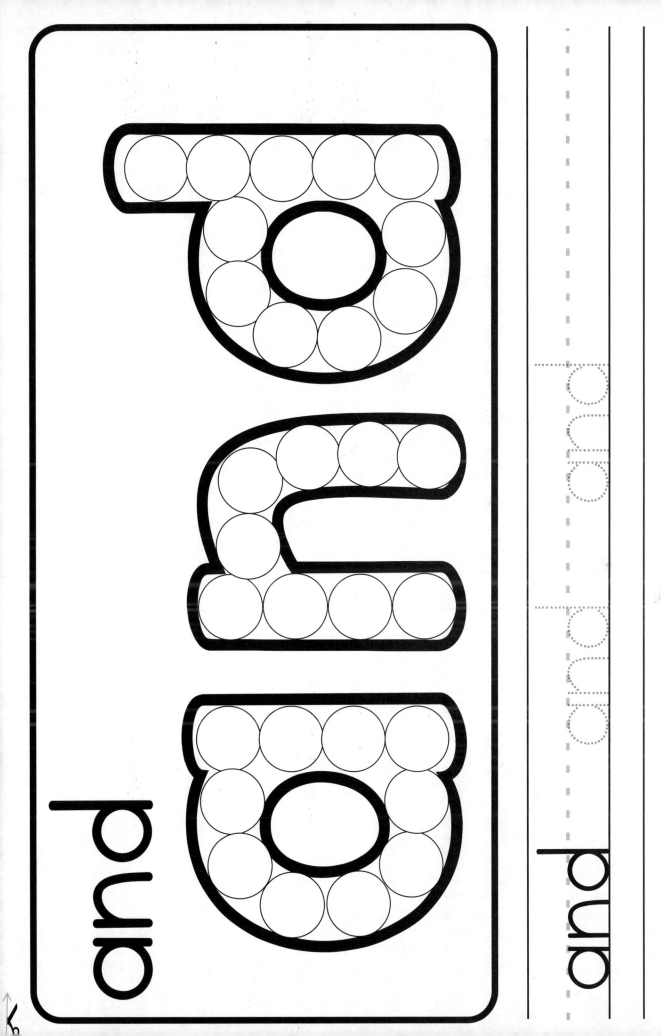

and

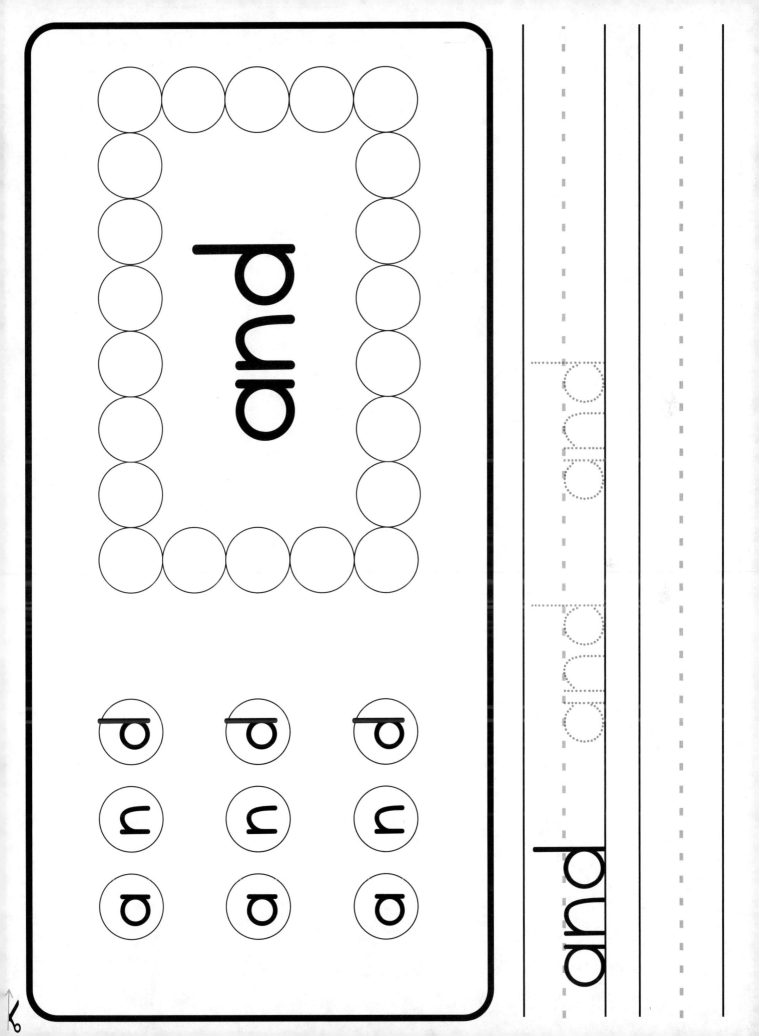

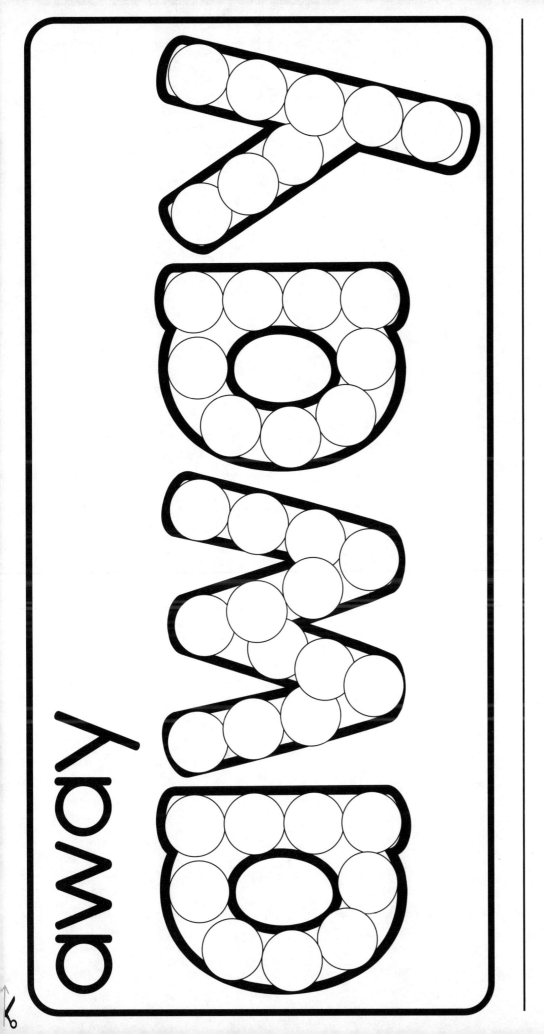

away

away away away

away

big

big big big

big

big

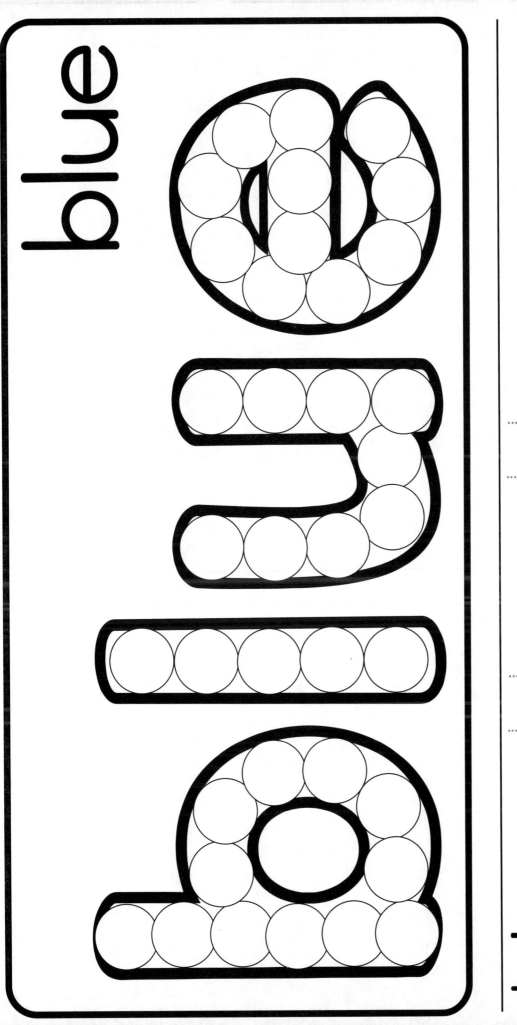

blue

blue blue blue

blue

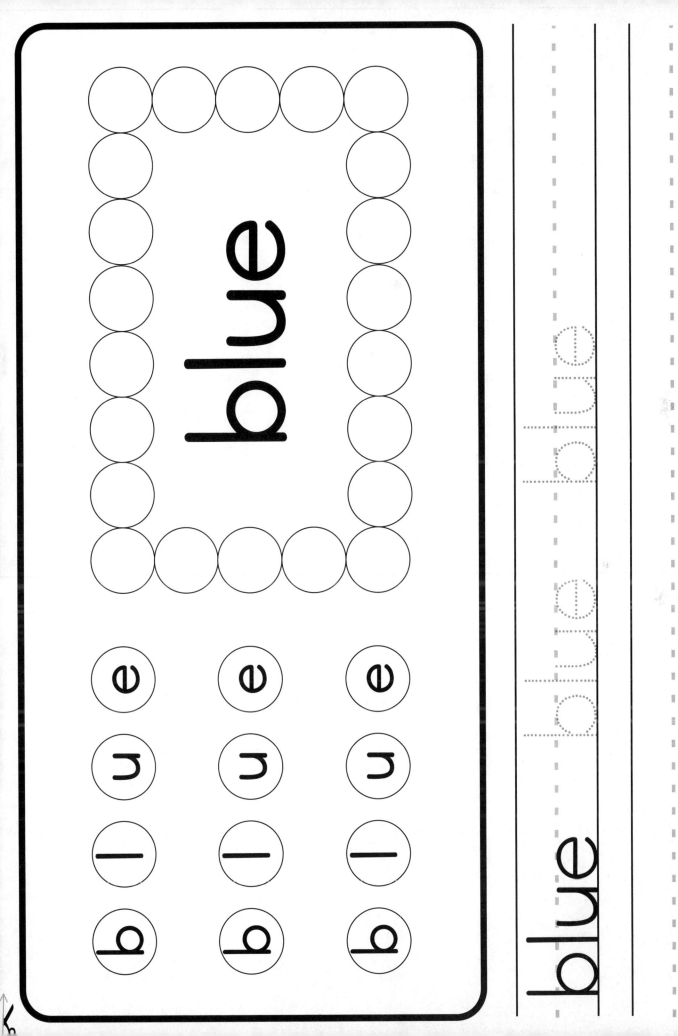

blue

can

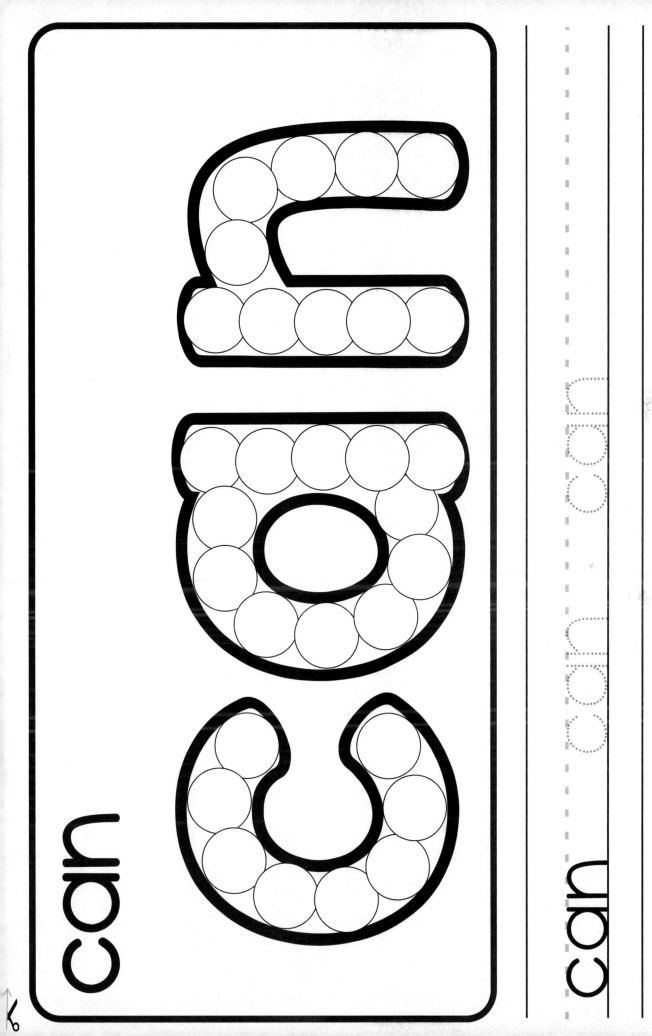

can   can   can

can

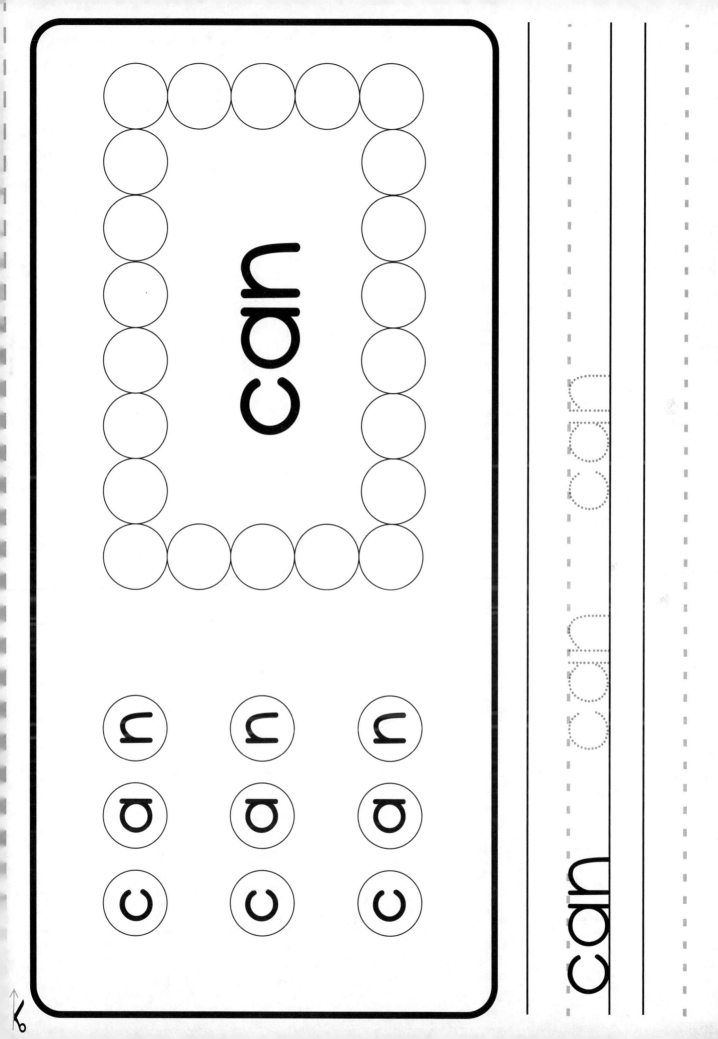

can

come

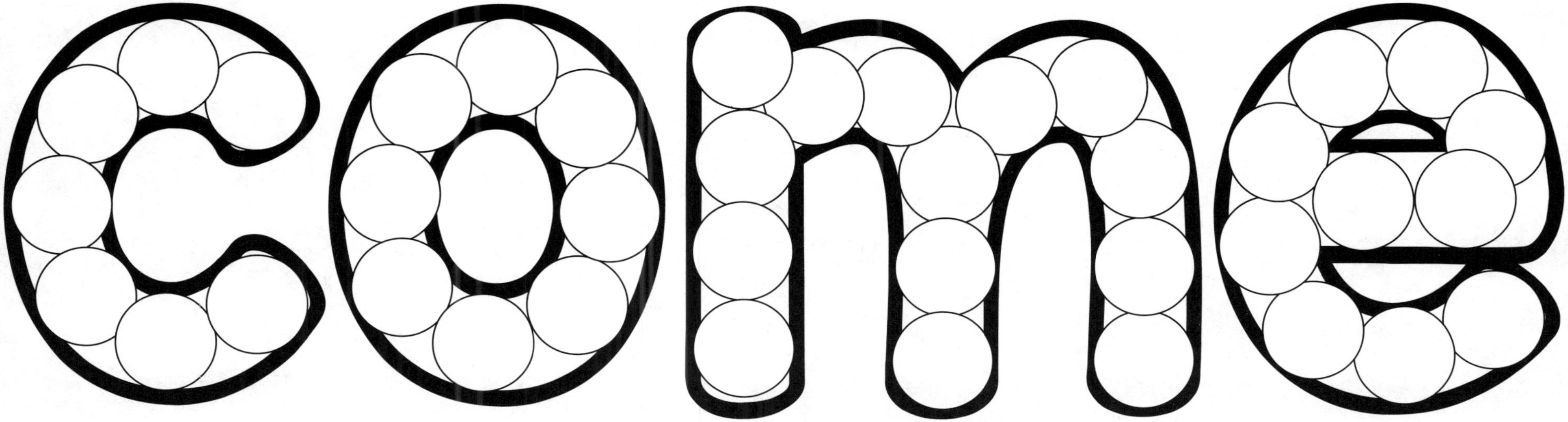

come

come come come

come

come

come come come

come

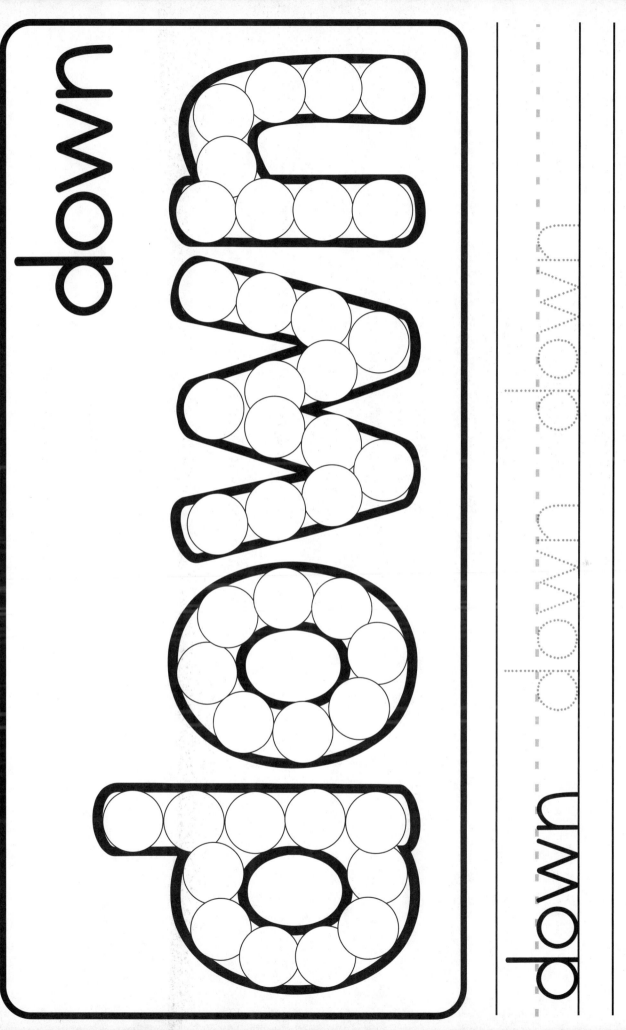

down

down

down down down

down

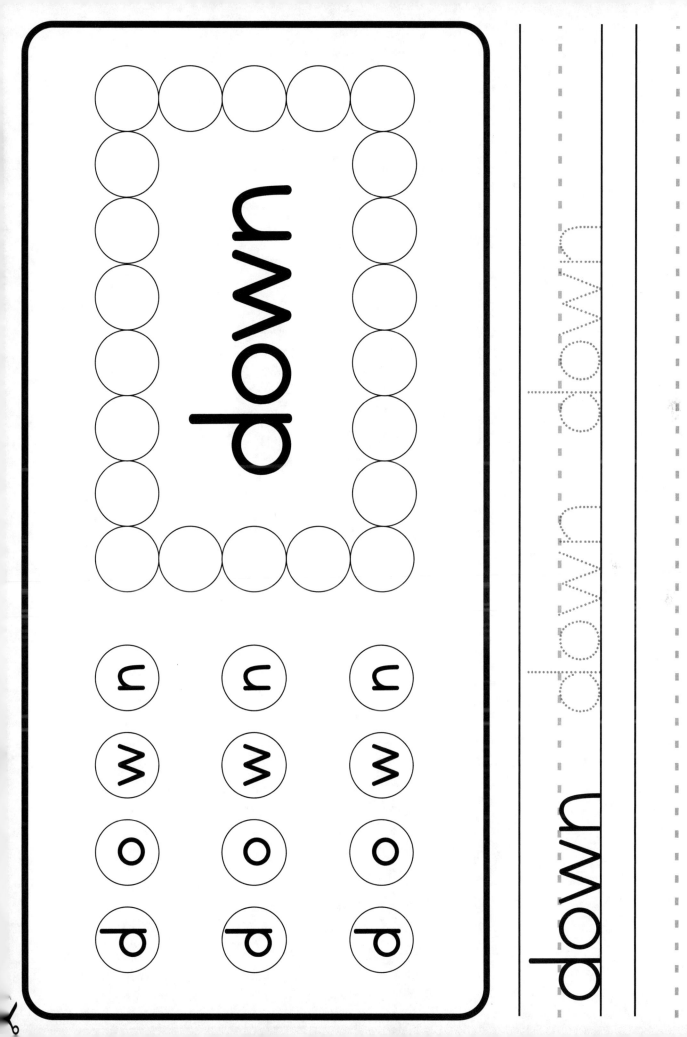

down

down down down

down

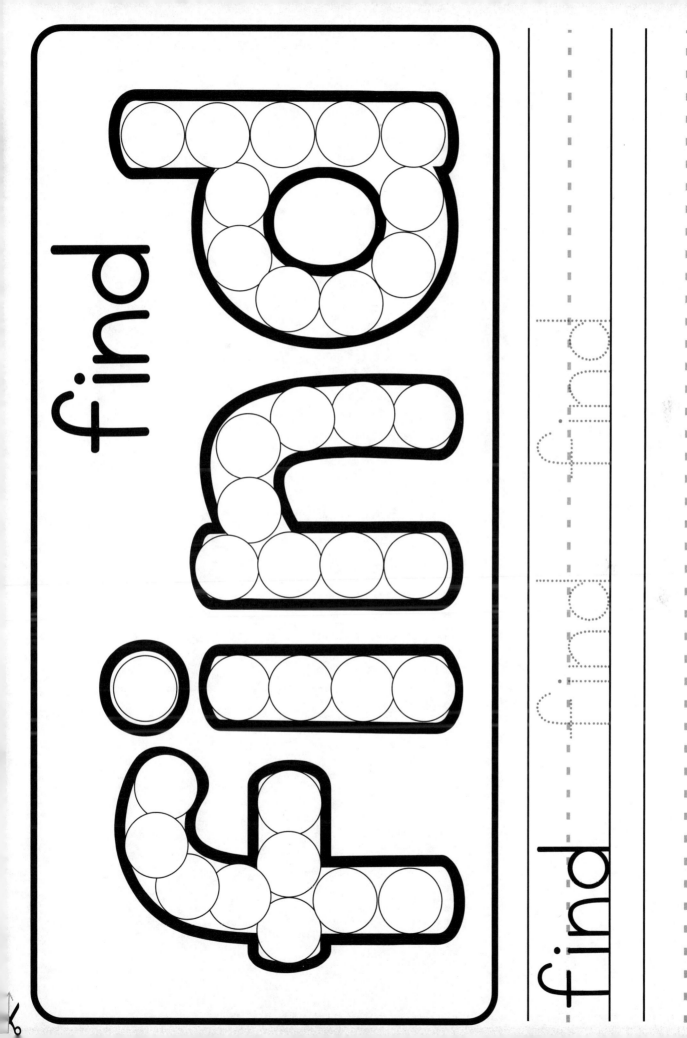

find

find

find

find

find

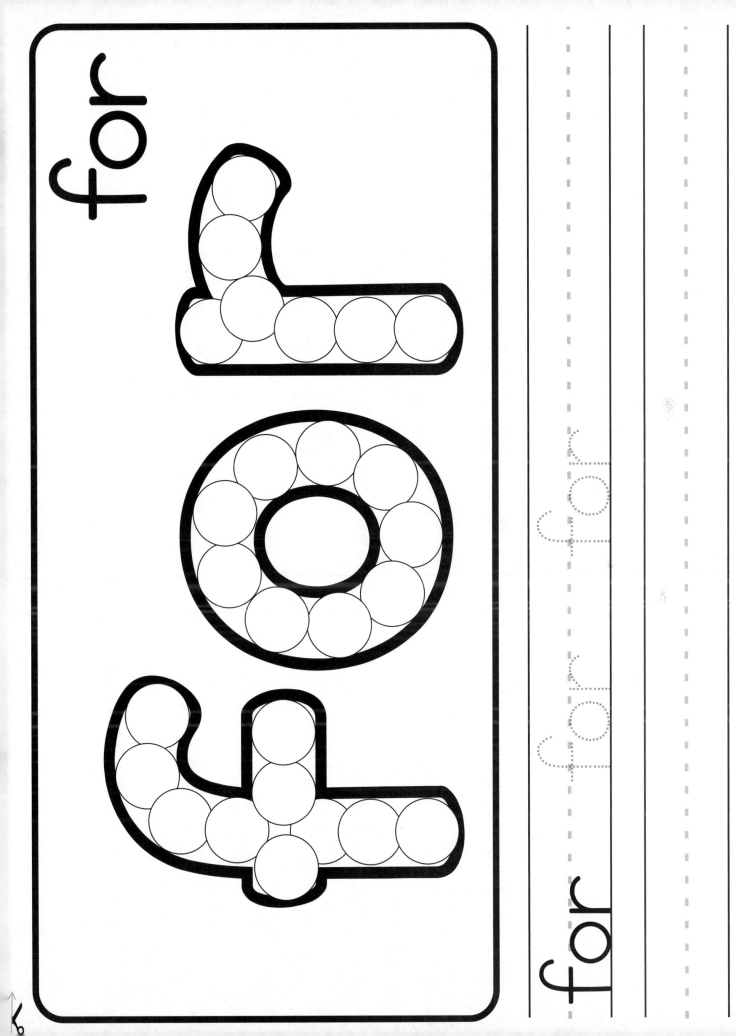

for

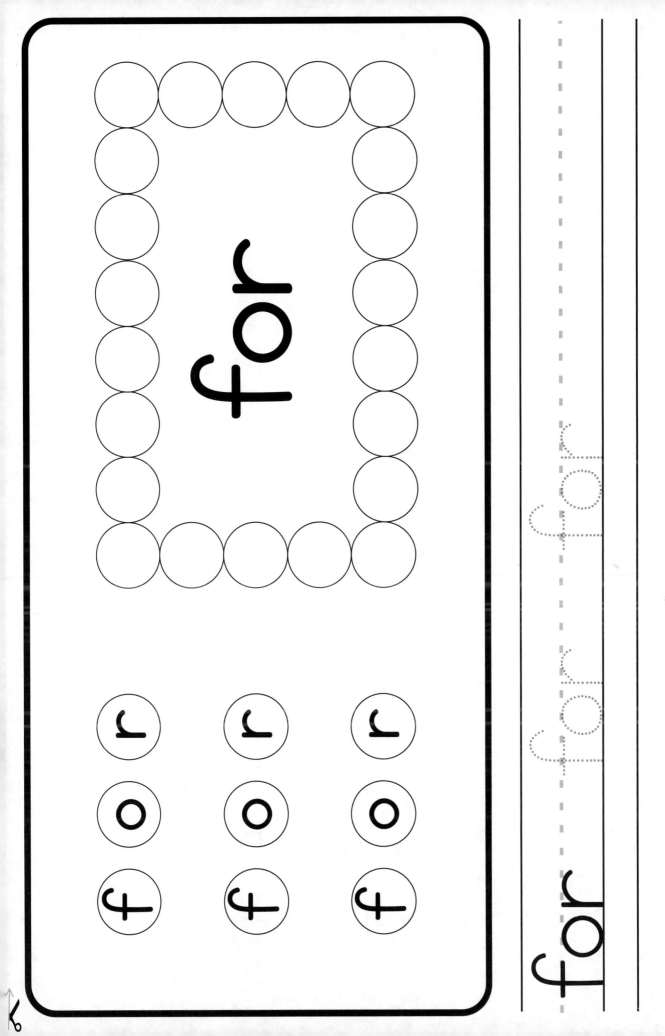

for

for

for for for

for

funny

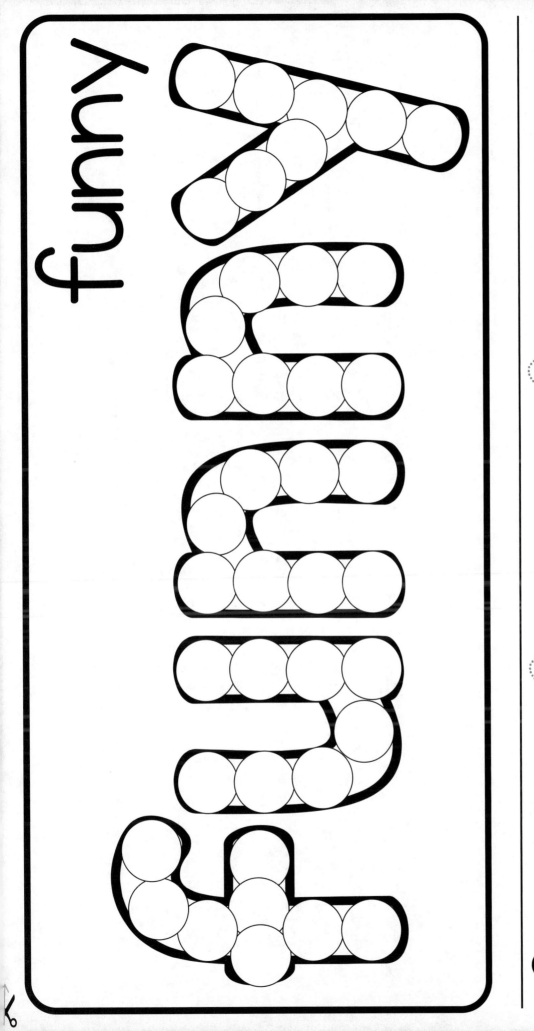

funny funny funny

funny

funny

funny

funny

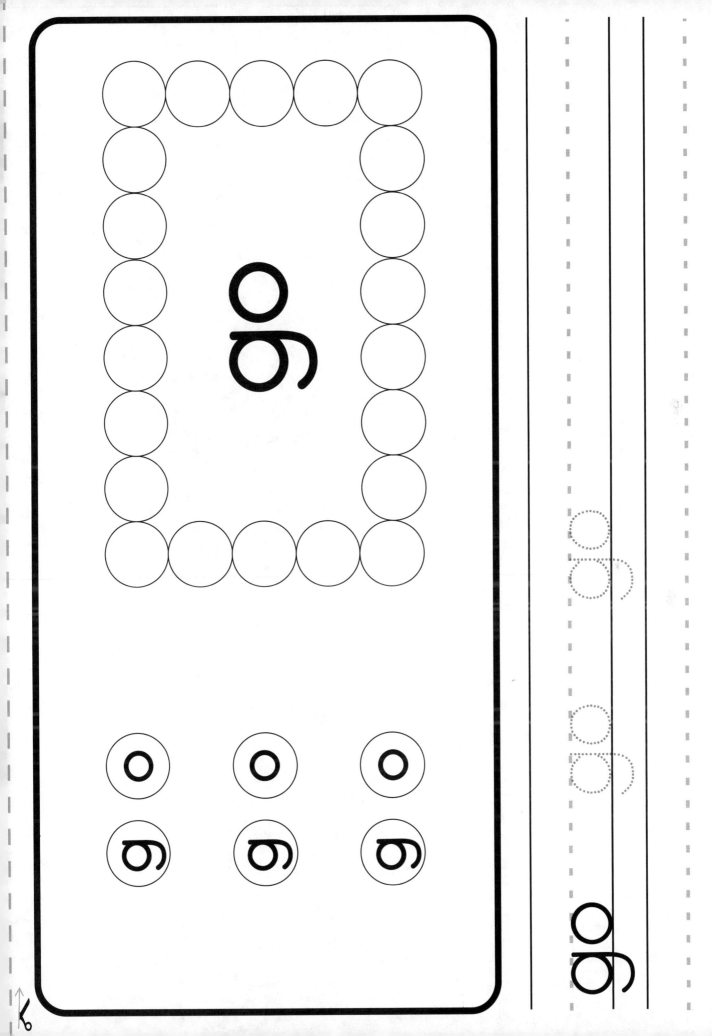

help

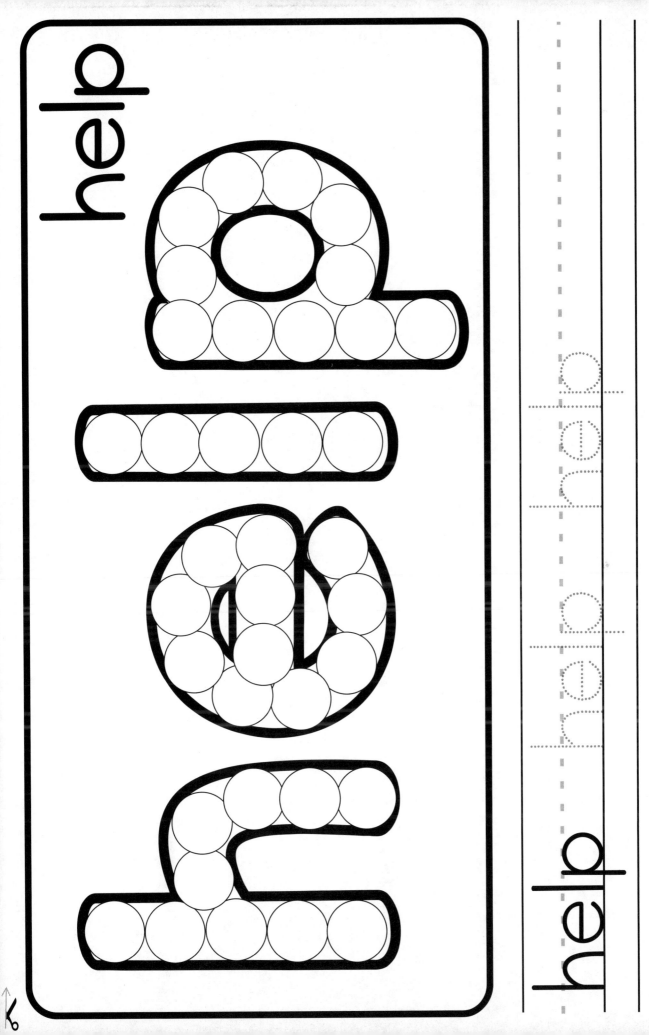

help help help

help

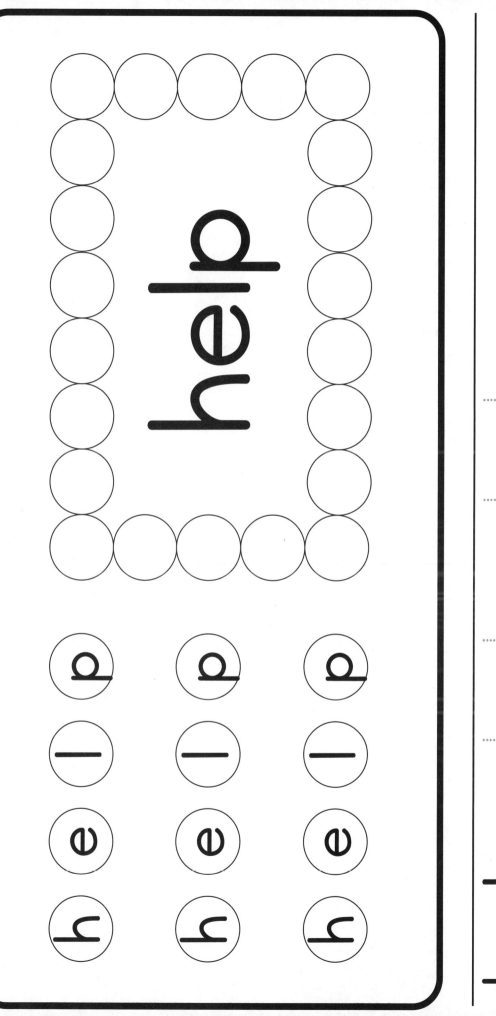

help

help

here

here

here here here

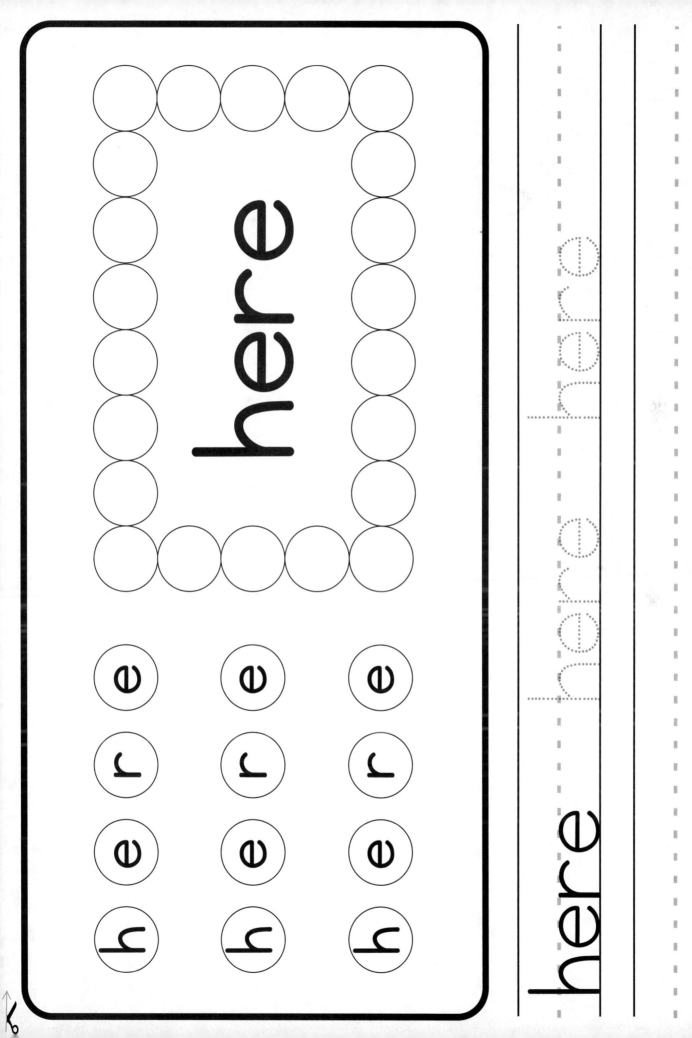

here

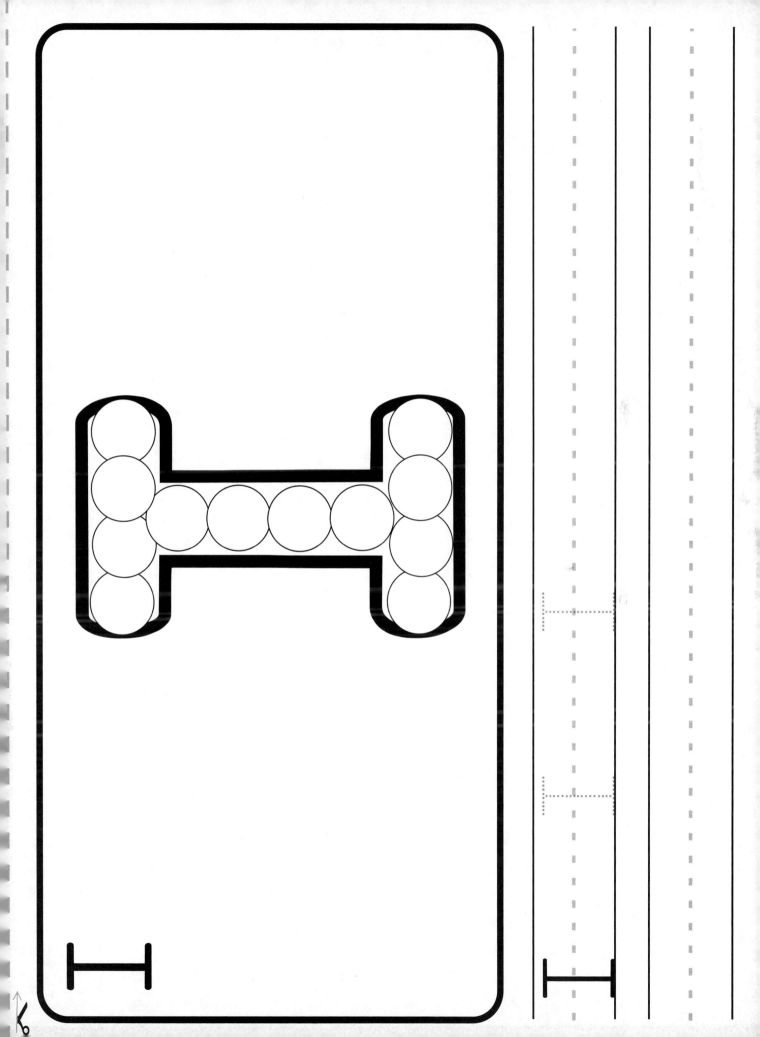

H

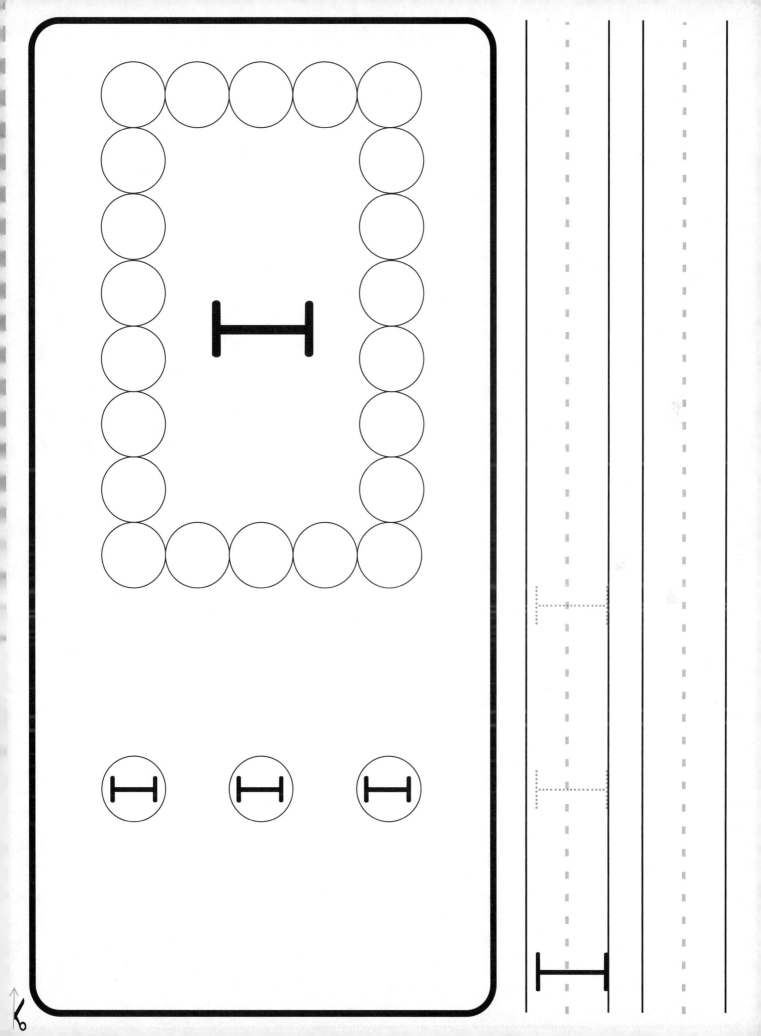

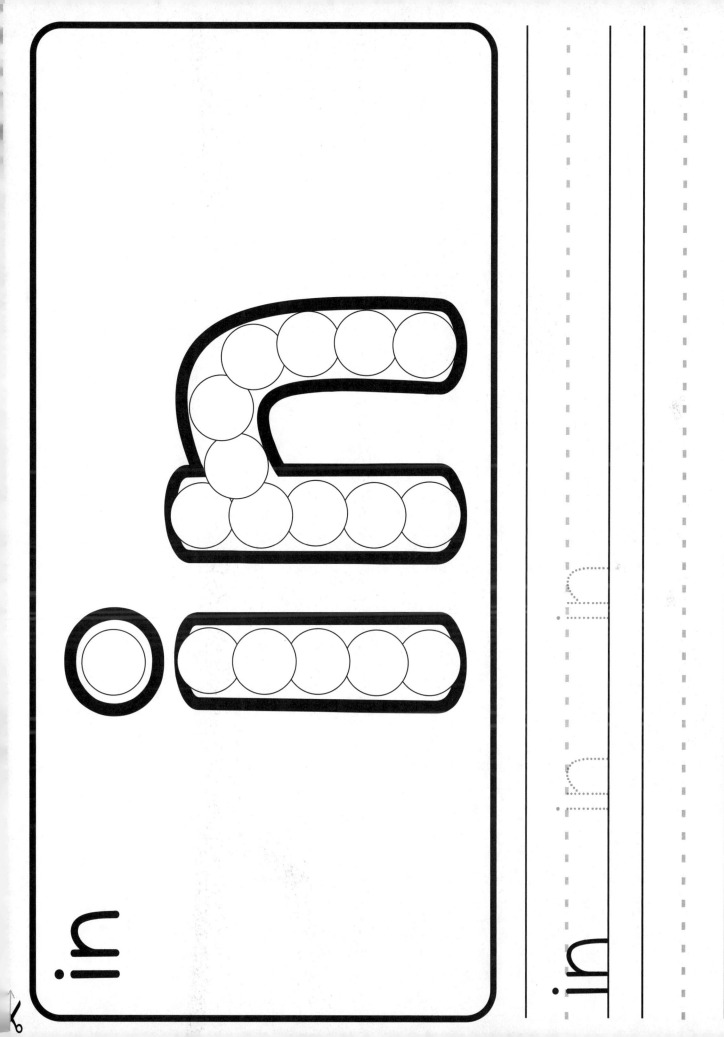

in

in

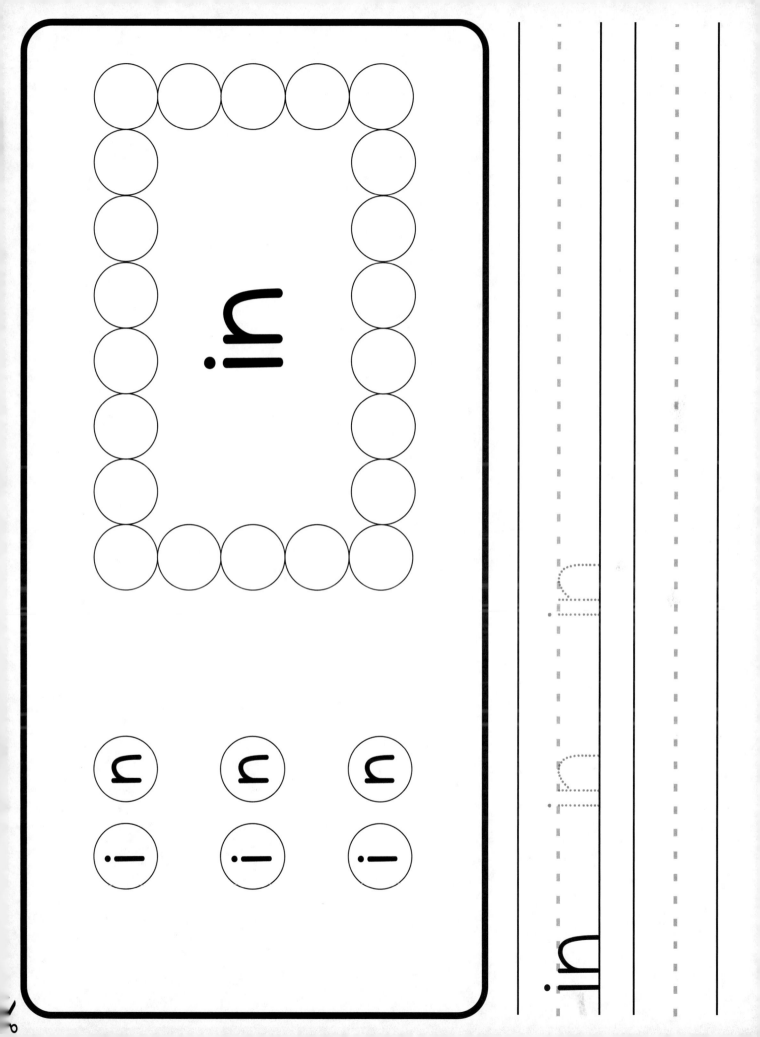

in

is

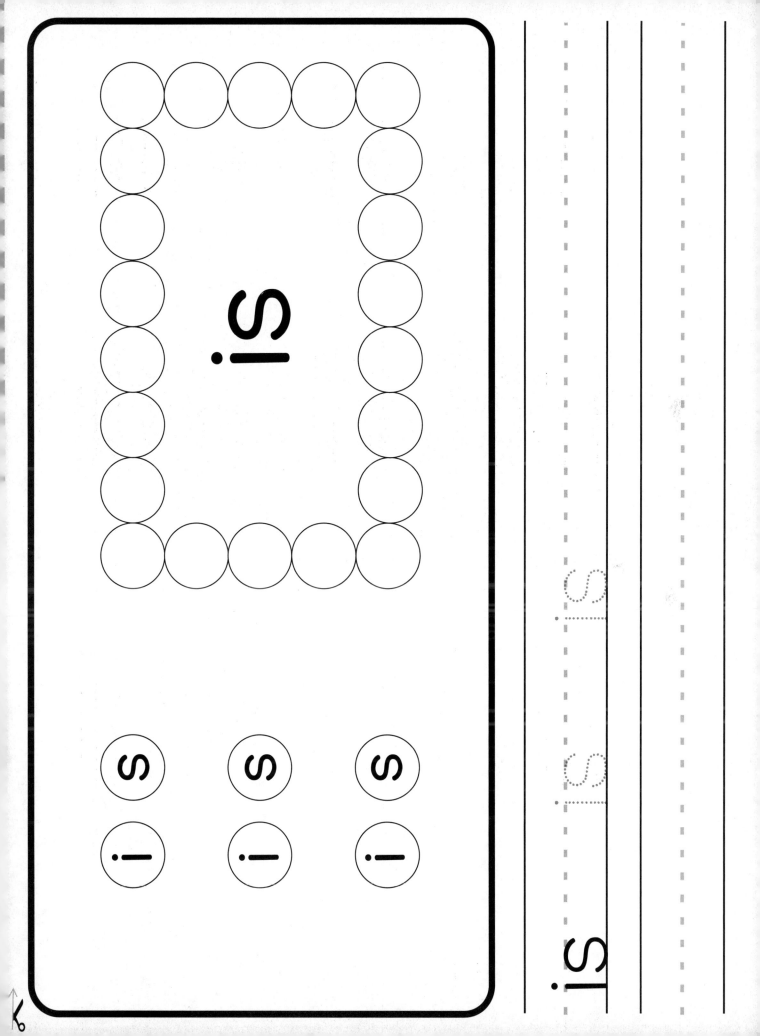

is

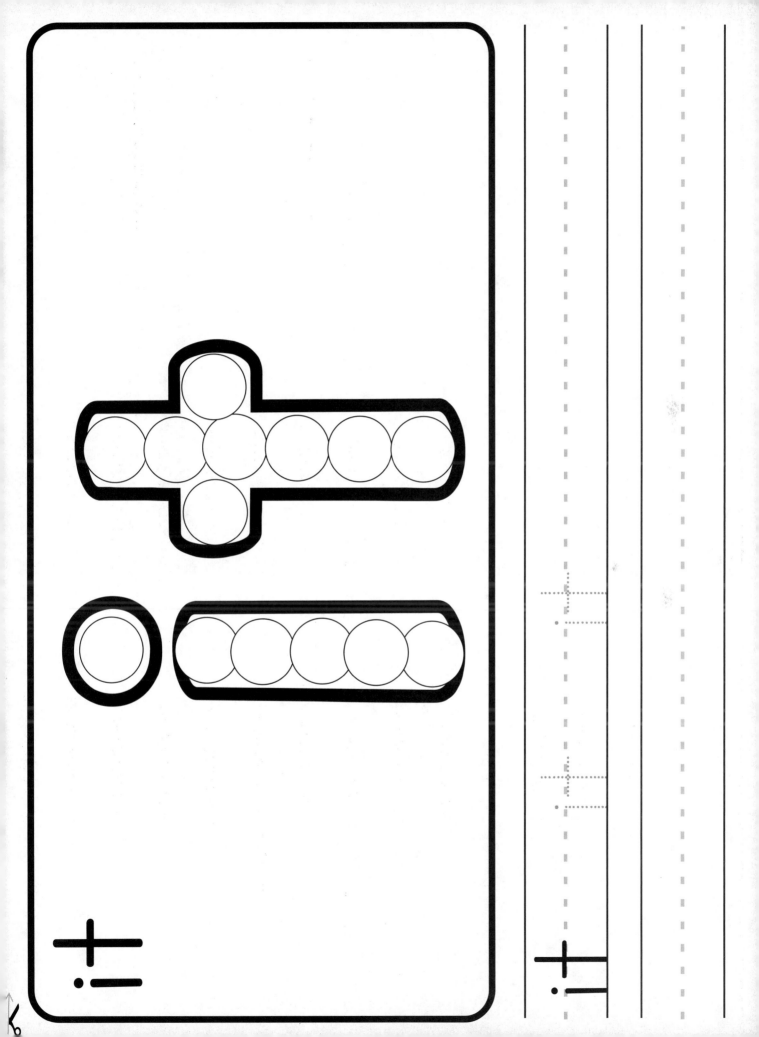

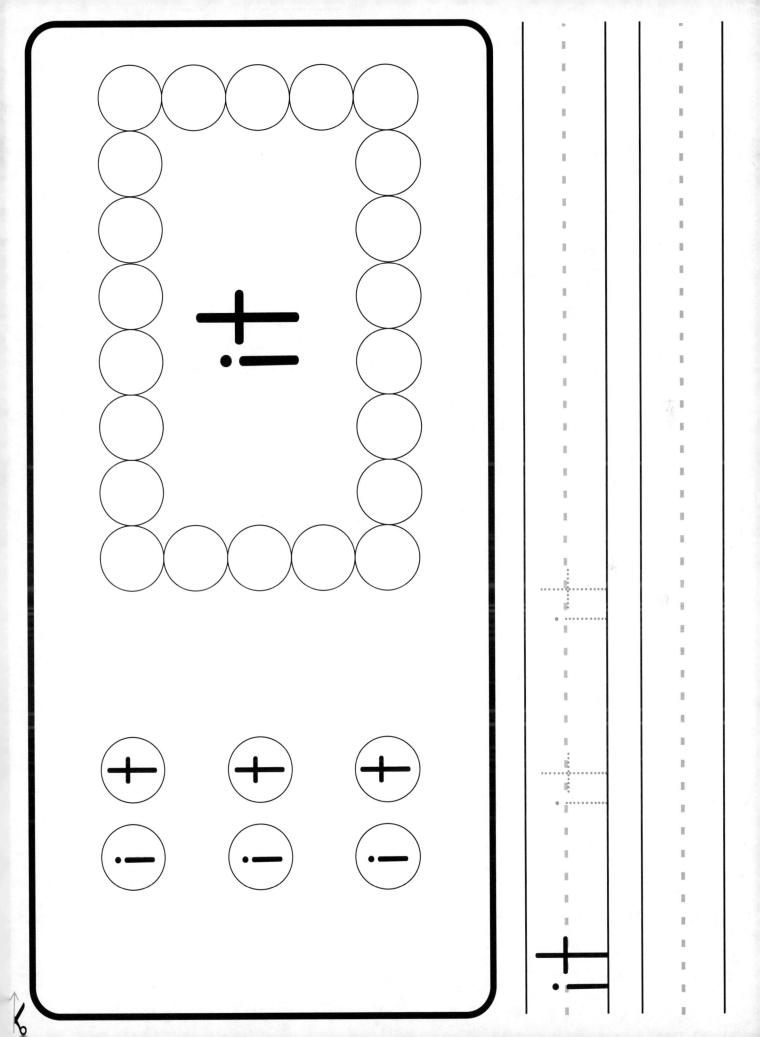

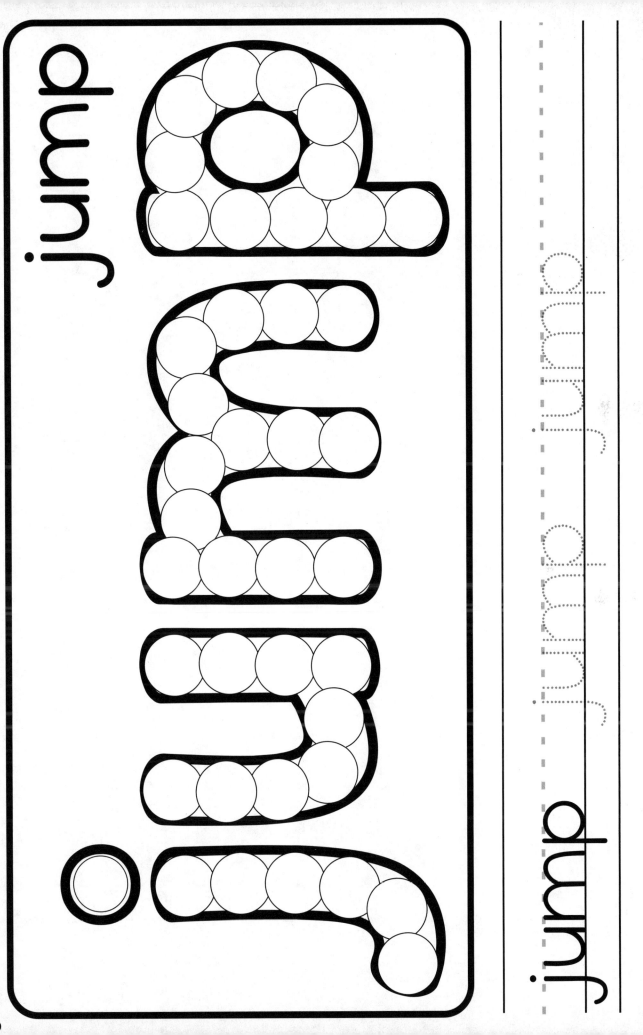

jump

jump jump jump

jump

jump

jump jump jump

jump

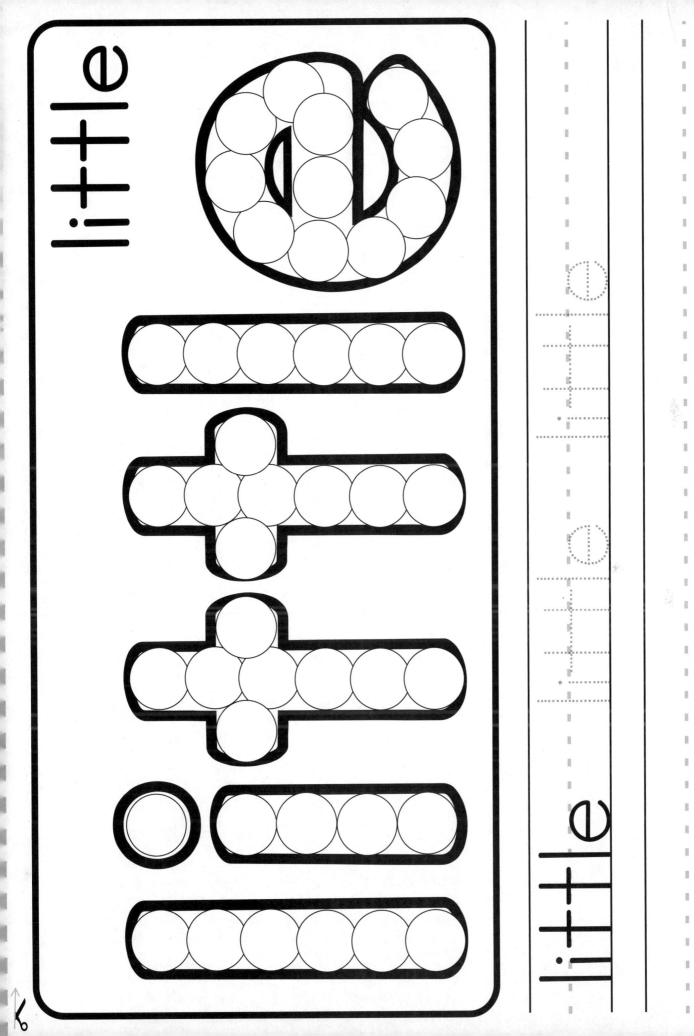

little

little

little

little

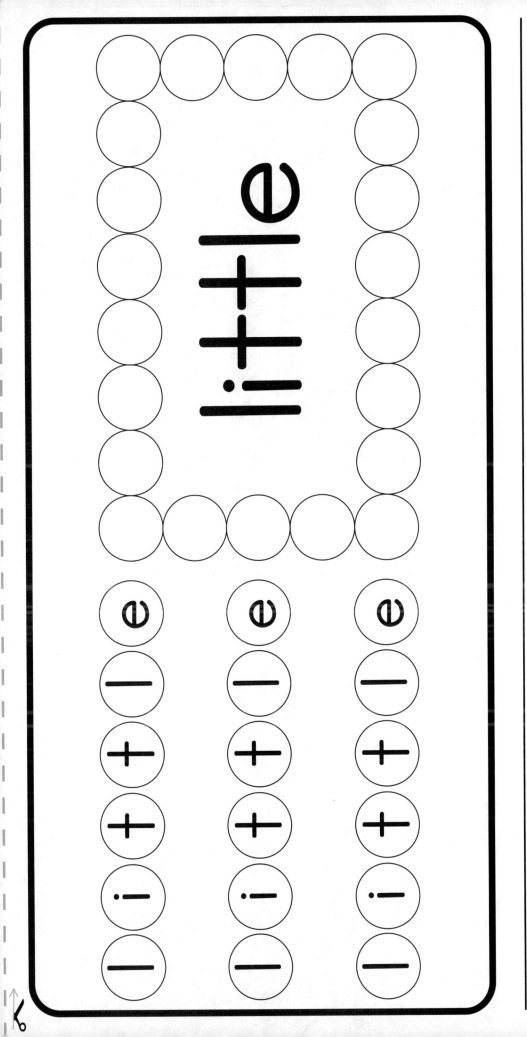

little little

little

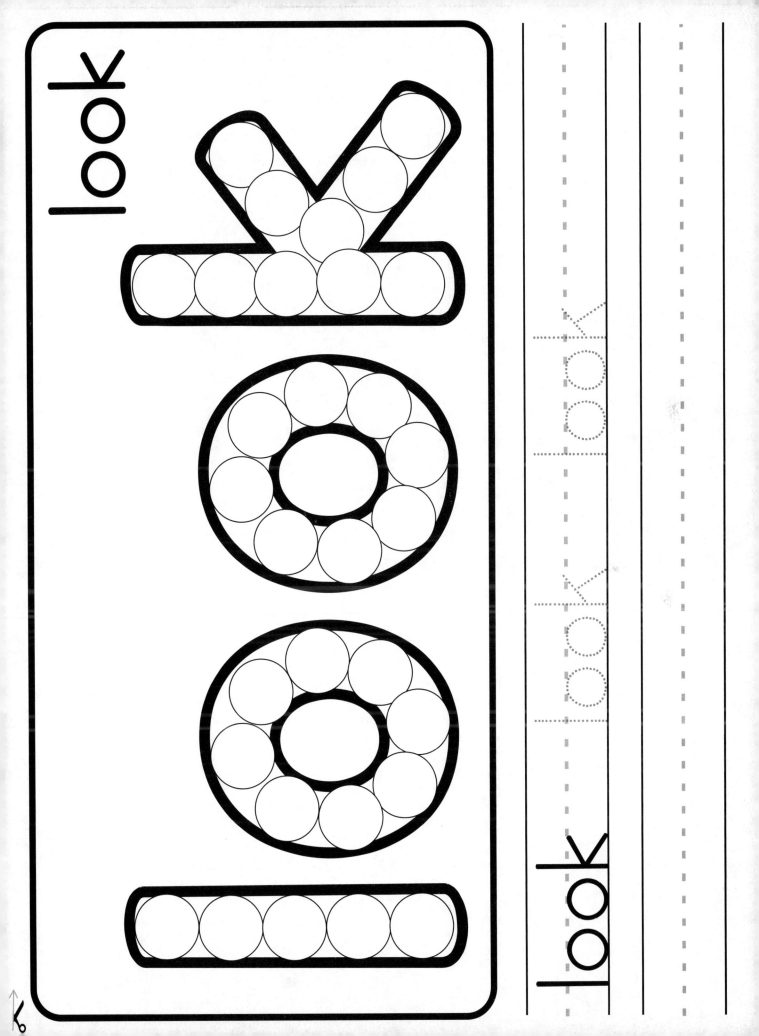

look

look look lok

look

make

make

make make make

make

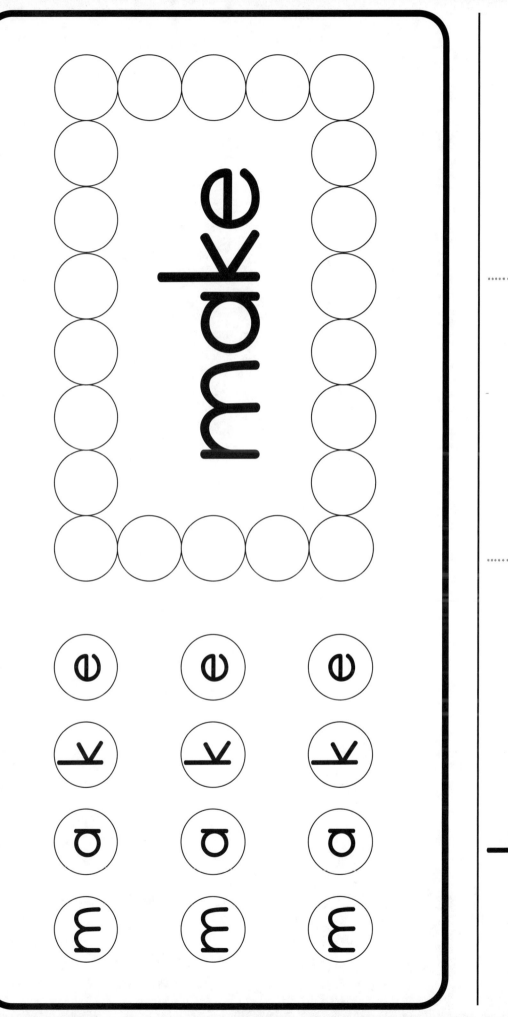

make

make make make

make

me

me

me   me

me

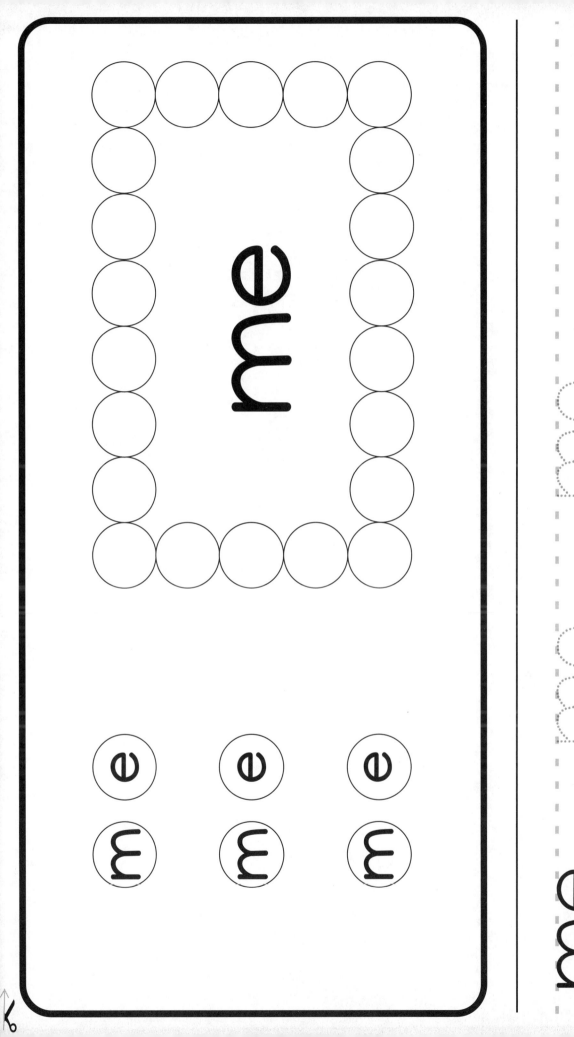

me

me me

me

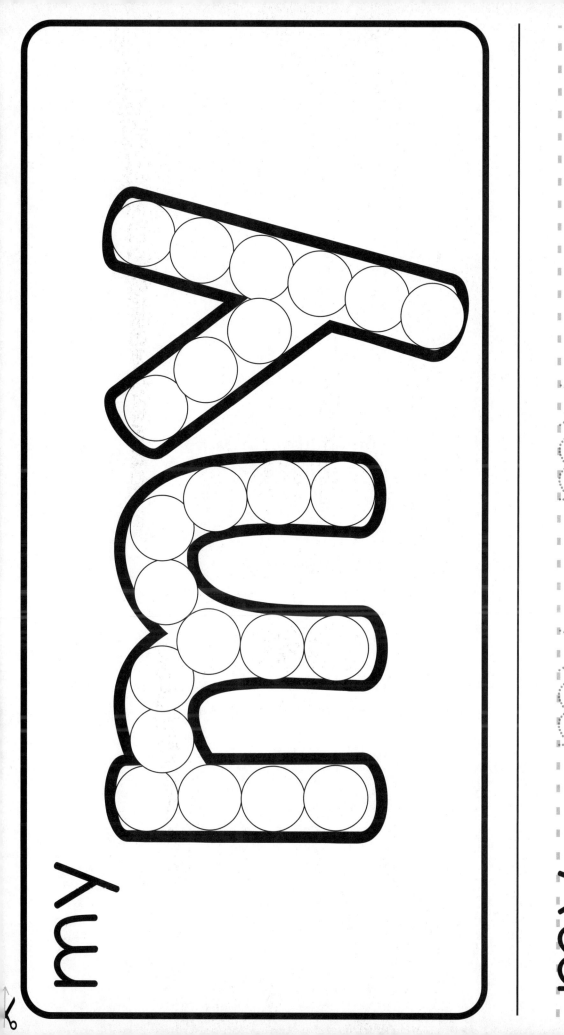

my

my

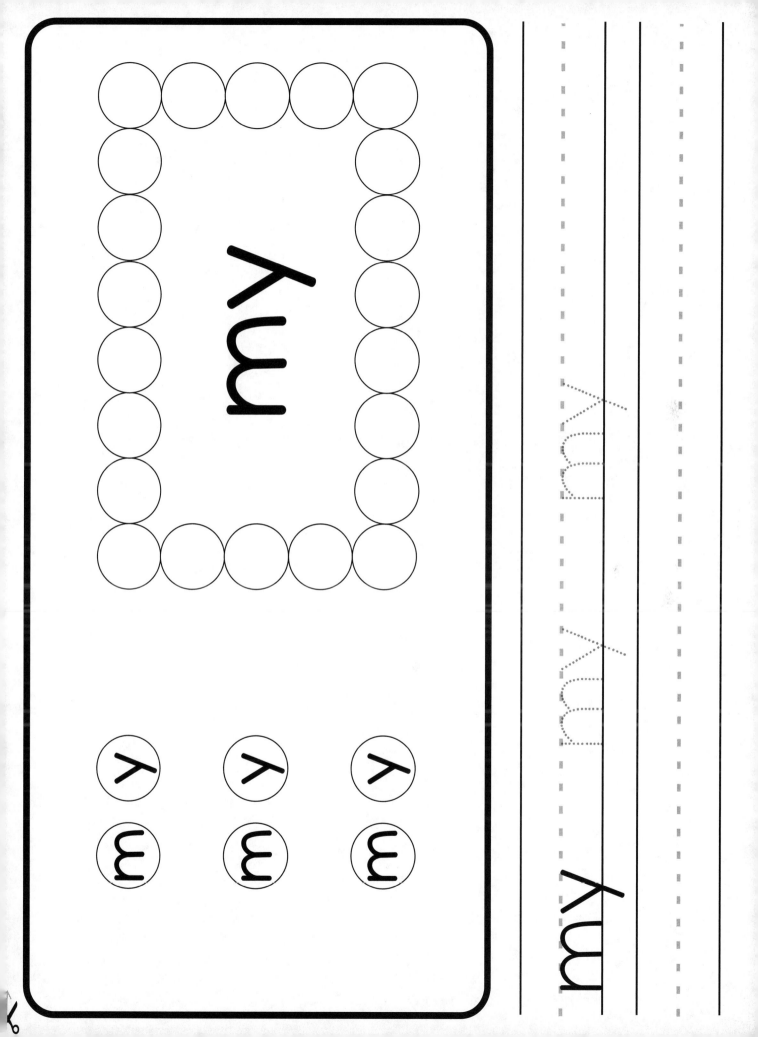

not

not

not

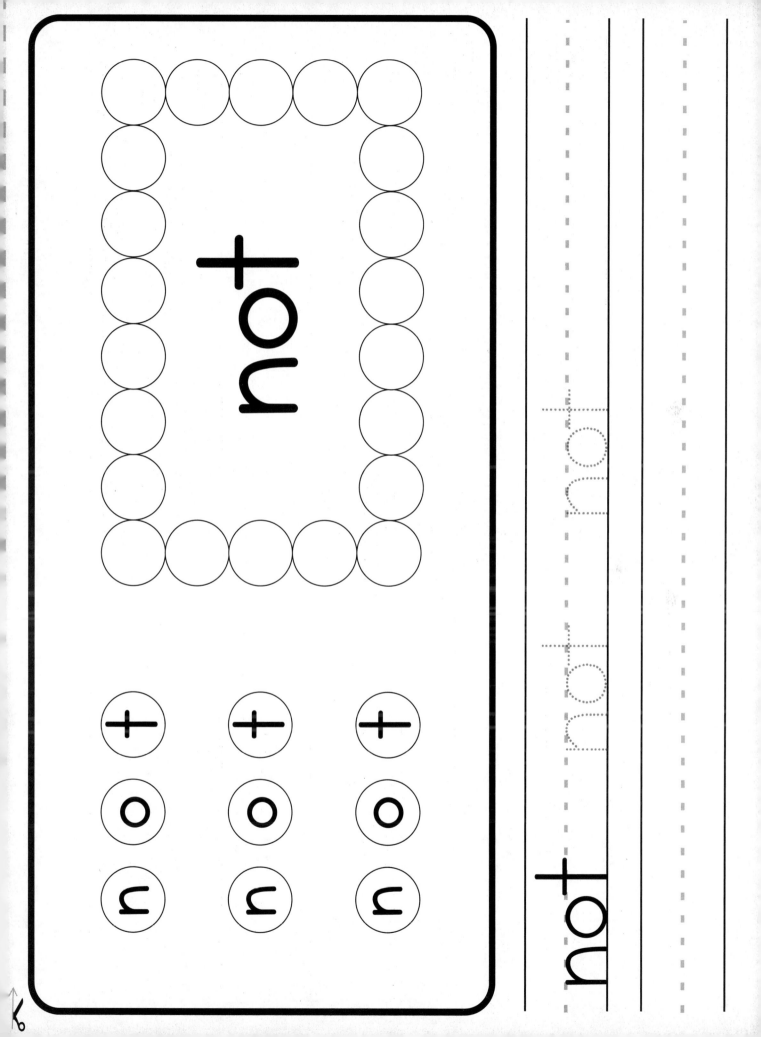

not

one

one

one one one
one

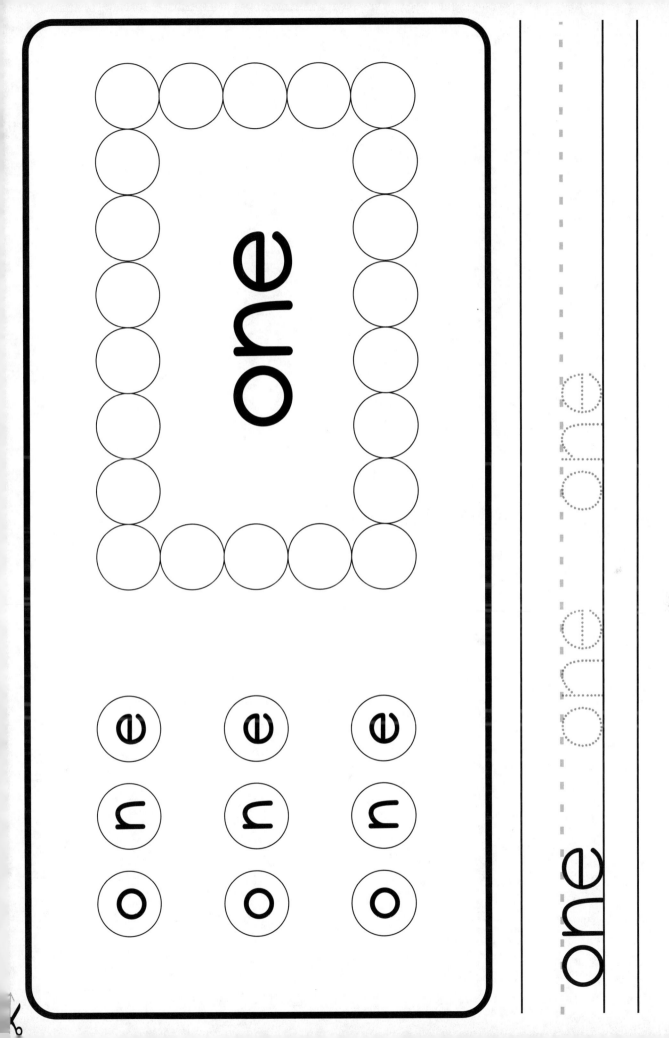

one

play

play play play

play

red

red red red

red red

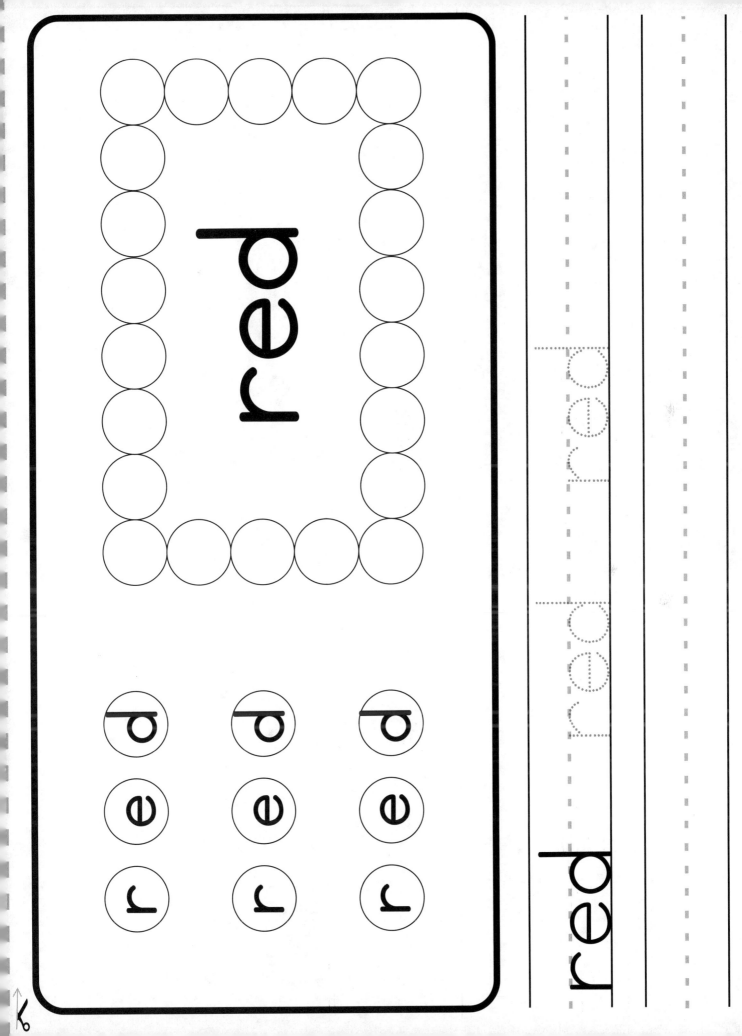

red

run

run run run

run

run

run run run

said

said

said said

said

said

said said said

said

see

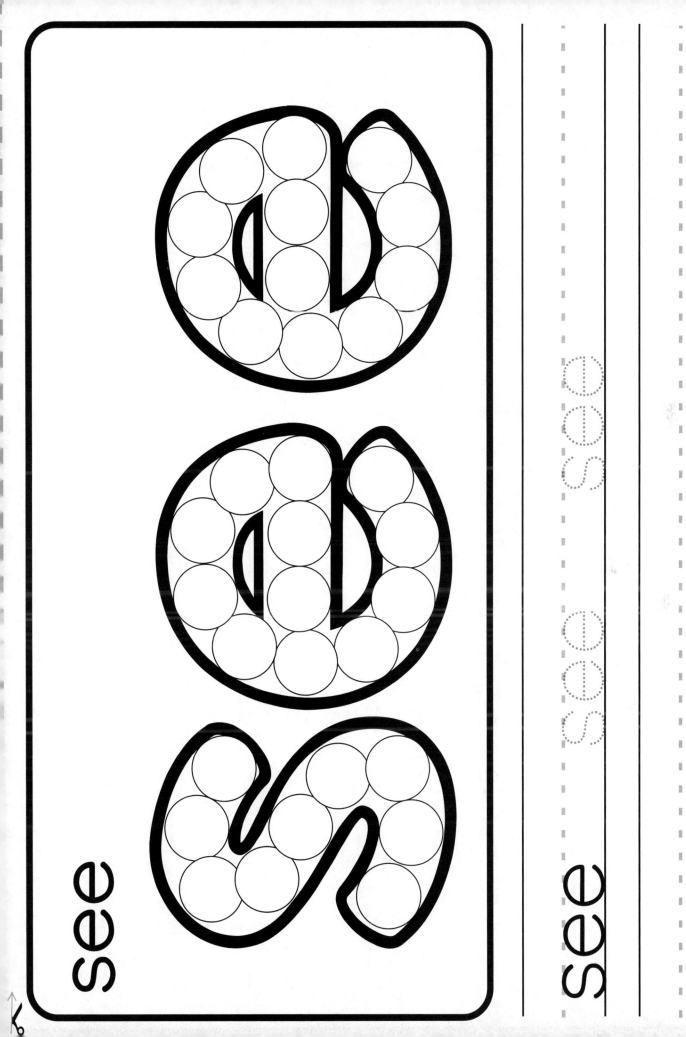

see

see

see

see

see

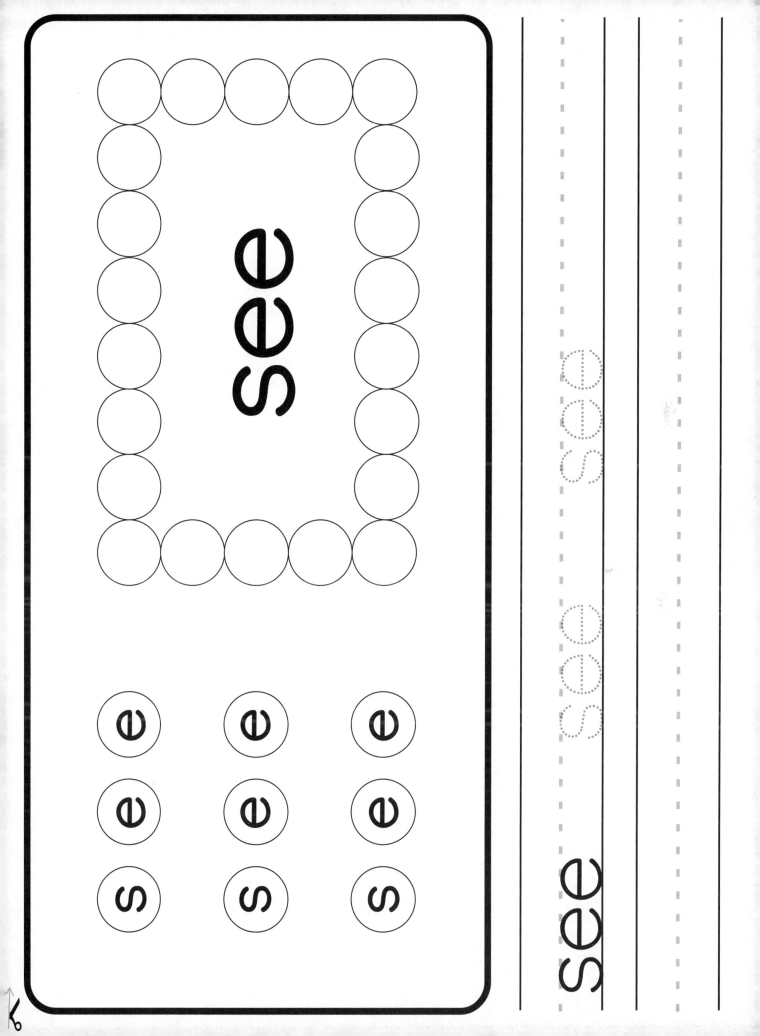

see

see see see

see

the

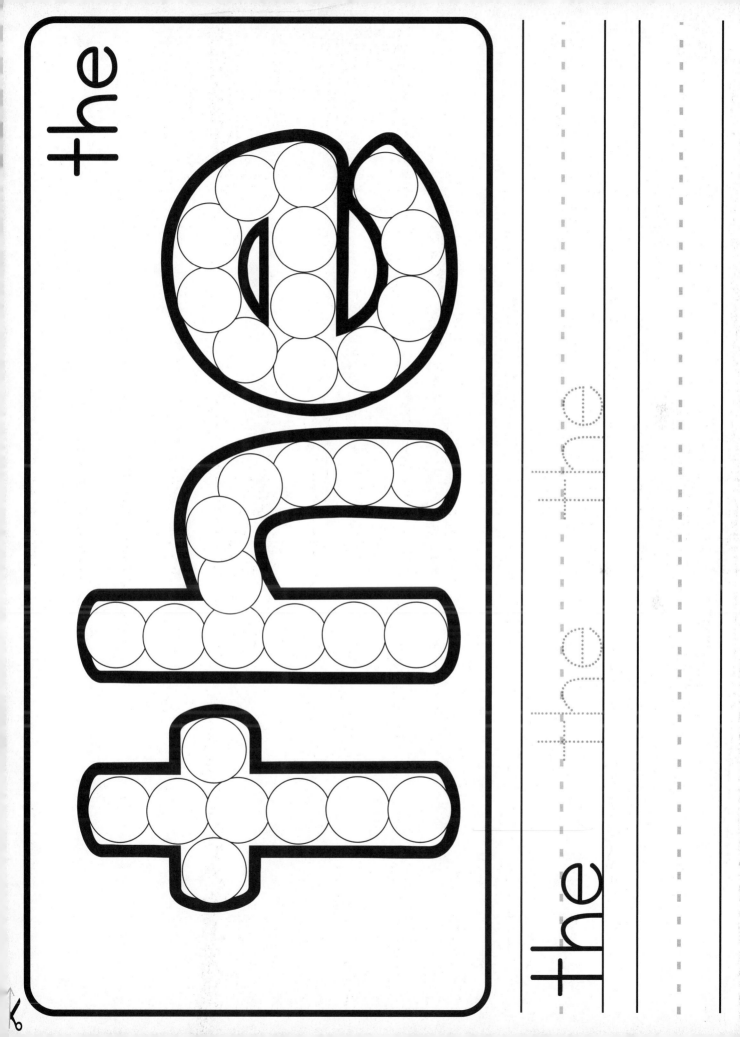

the the the

the

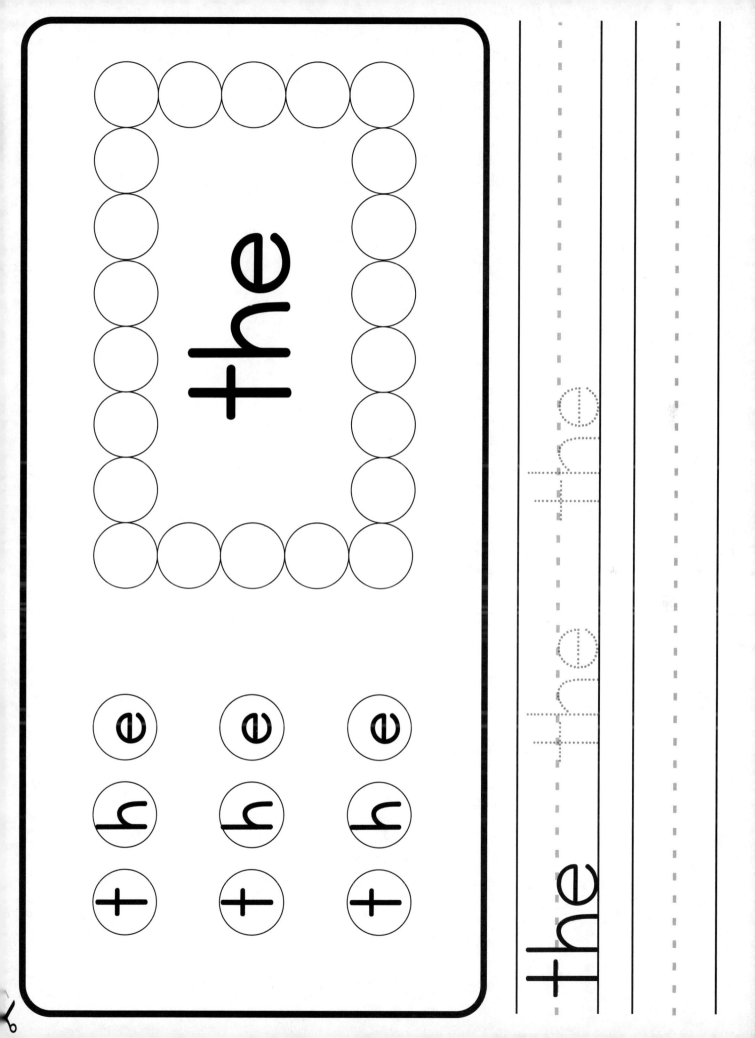

three

three three

three

three

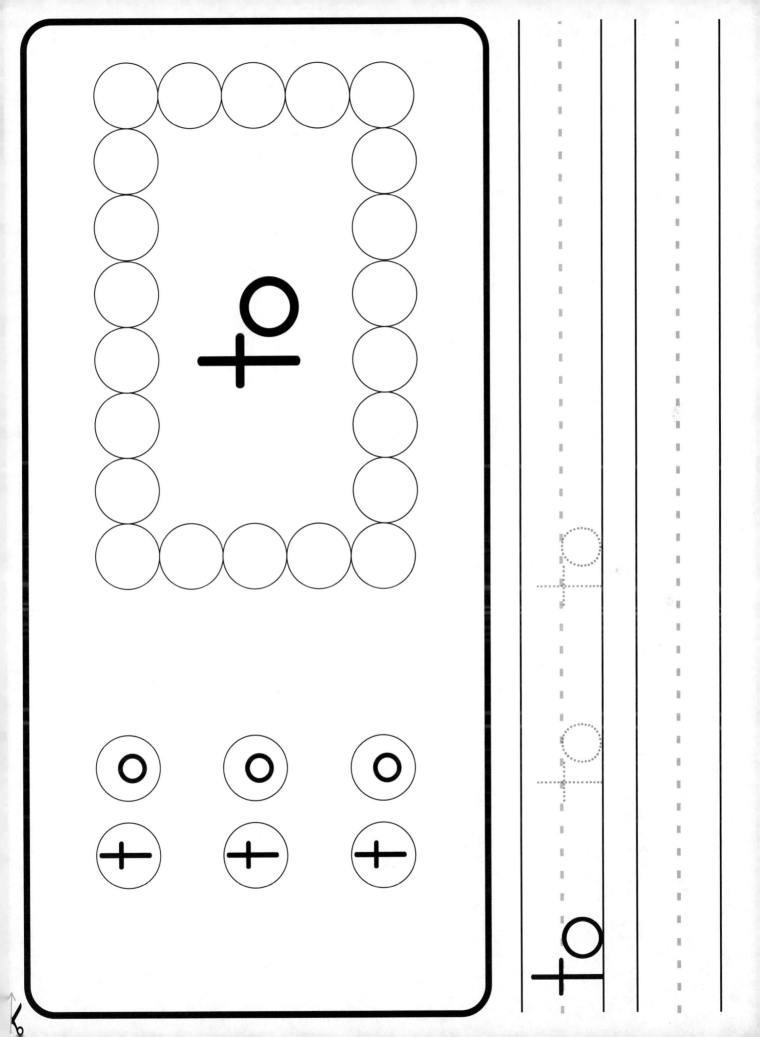

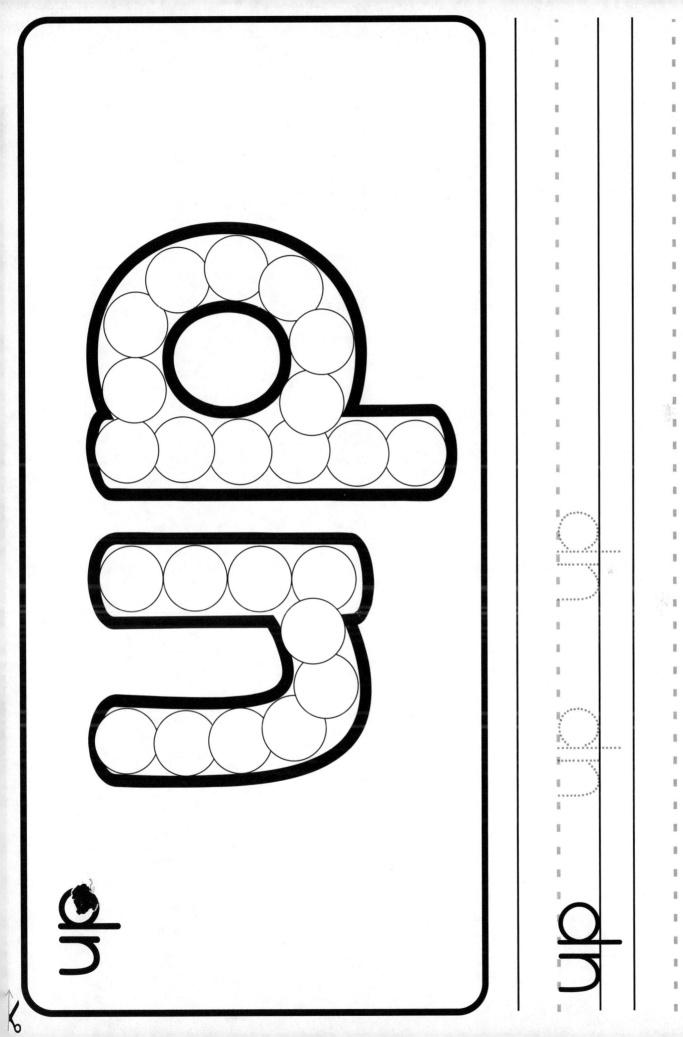

up

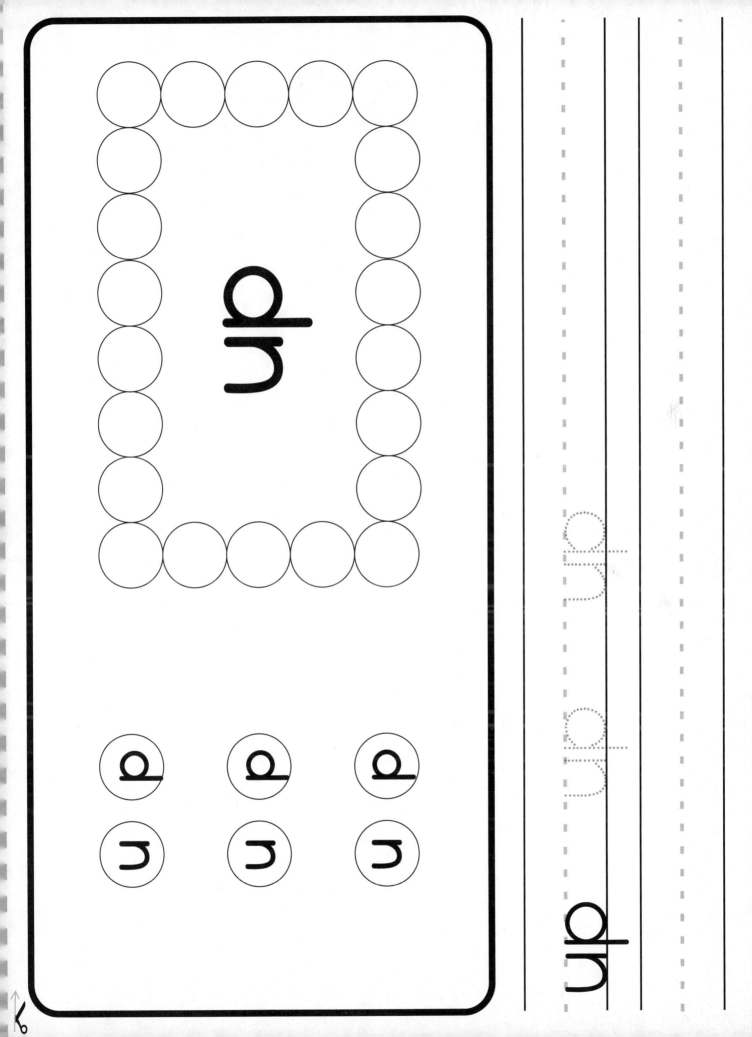

up

we

we we we

we

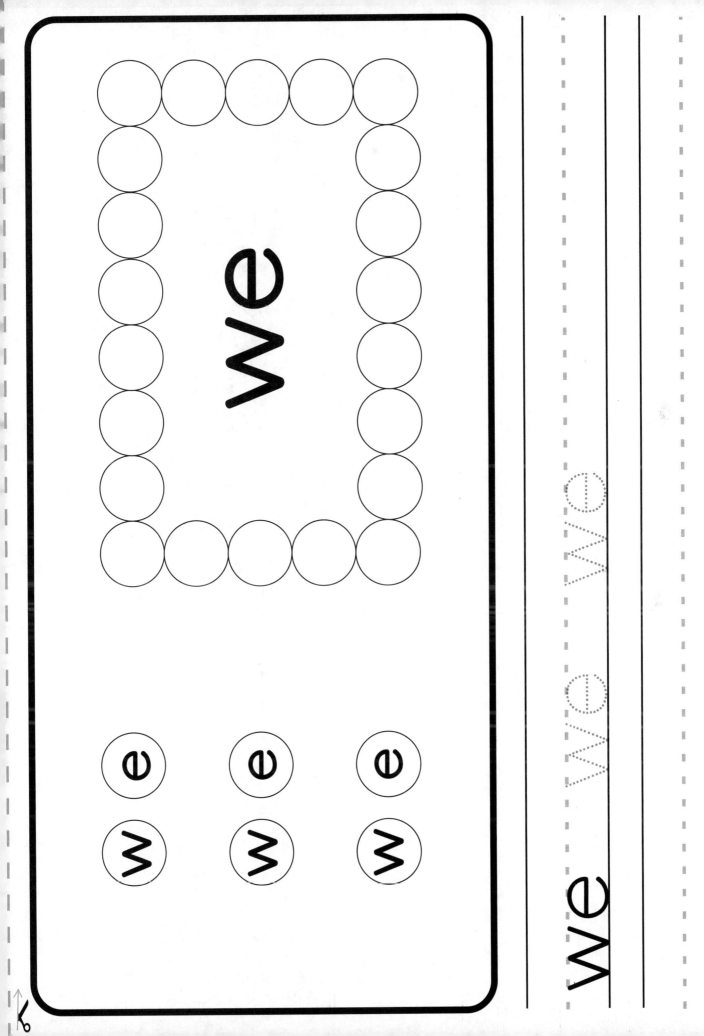

we

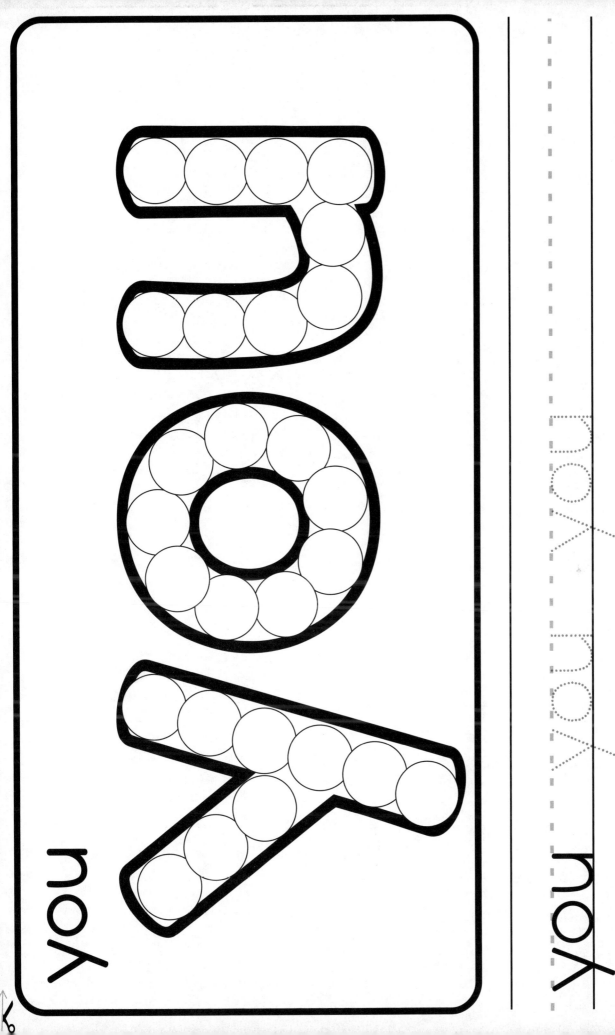

you

you you you

you

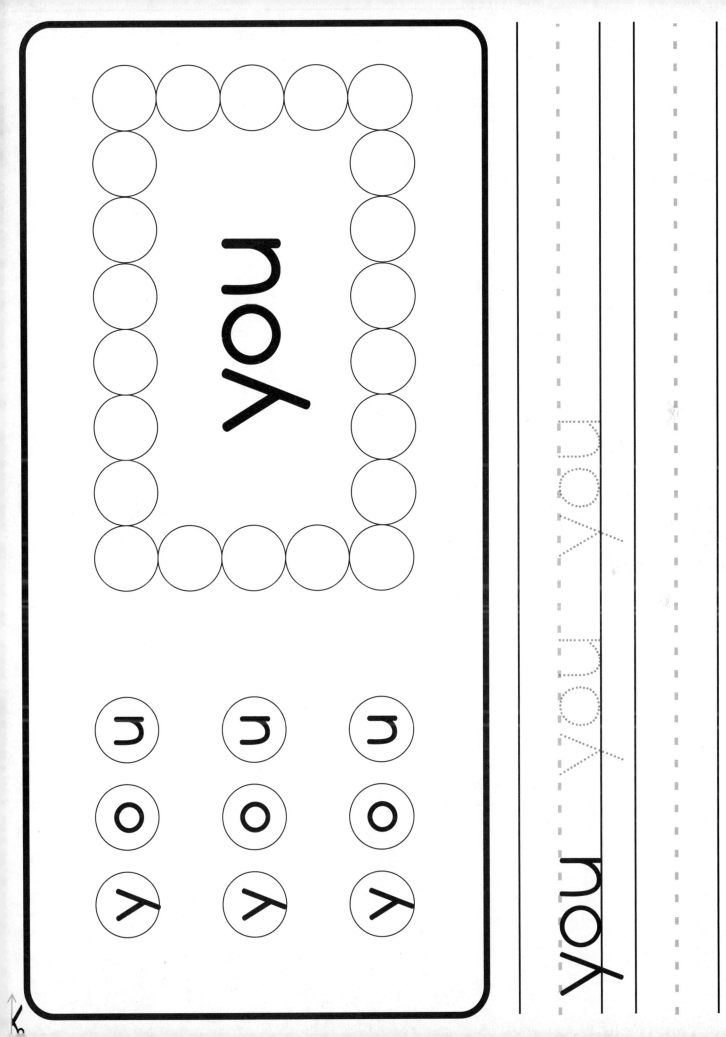

Ages 3+

Pre-K Skills Series Book 4

Numbers & Counting

READY FOR Preschool

Dot Markers Activity Book

With BIG DOT Circles

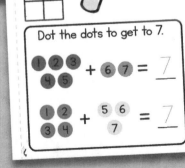

Black reverse pages for less bleed-through!

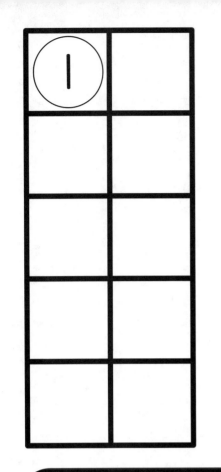  

one

Dot the dots to get to 1.

0 + 1 = __

1 + 0 = __

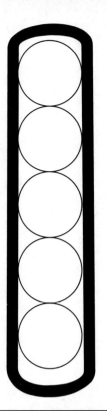

Count and dot
the one sun.

one

1

Find and dot all the number 1's.

3	1	5	4	1
2	1	4	6	8
7	0	1	5	0
1	5	9	0	2
1	3	0	9	1

two

Dot the dots to get to 2.

① + ② = 2

①② + 0 = 2

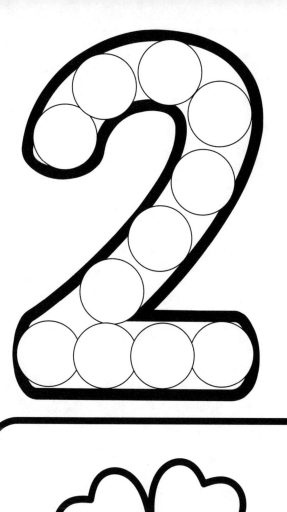

Count and dot the
two middles
of the flowers.

two 2

Find and dot all the number 2's.

2	0	3	9	7
2	1	2	3	2
7	0	8	5	0
6	2	1	2	8
4	1	0	9	2

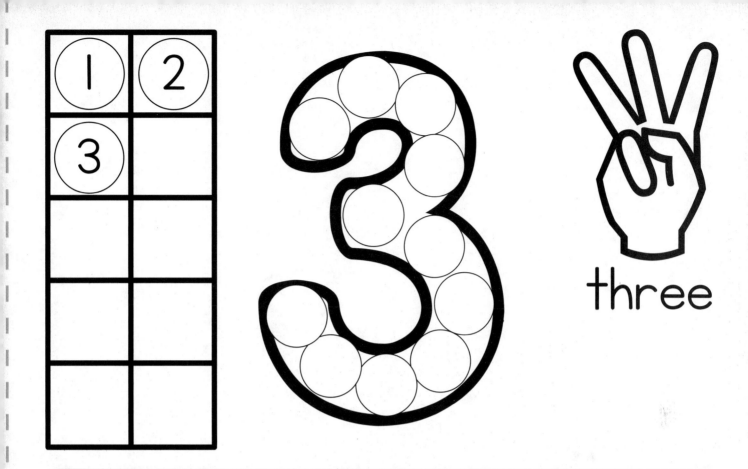

Dot the dots to get to 3.

①② + ③ = 3 _____

① + ②③ = 3 _____

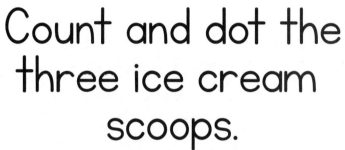

Count and dot the three ice cream scoops.

three  3

Find and dot all the number 3's.

0	3	1	8	7
3	0	2	1	2
7	0	9	3	0
9	3	4	2	4
2	5	1	0	3

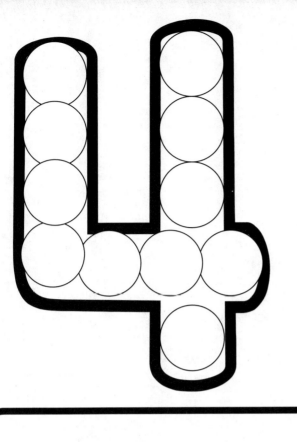

Count and dot
the four clouds.

____

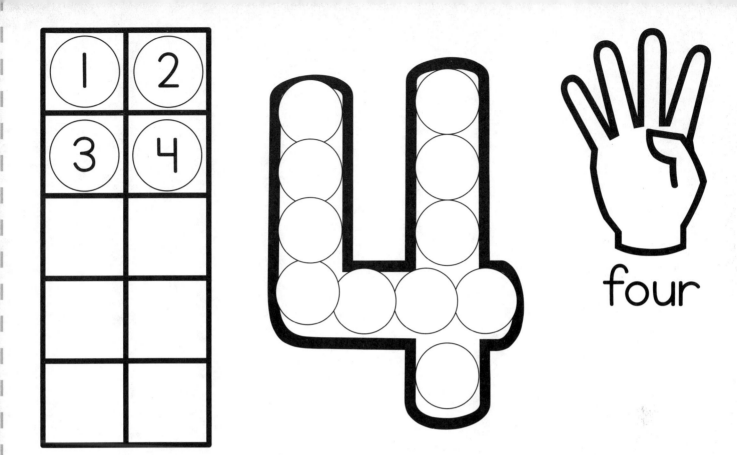

four

Dot the dots to get to 4.

$\left(1\right)\left(2\right) + \left(3\right)\left(4\right) = \underline{}$

$\left(1\right)\left(2\right)\left(3\right) + \left(4\right) = \underline{}$

four

Find and dot all the number 4's.

4	0	0	9	8
7	0	3	4	1
4	4	5	3	0
9	8	4	2	4
7	5	1	6	2

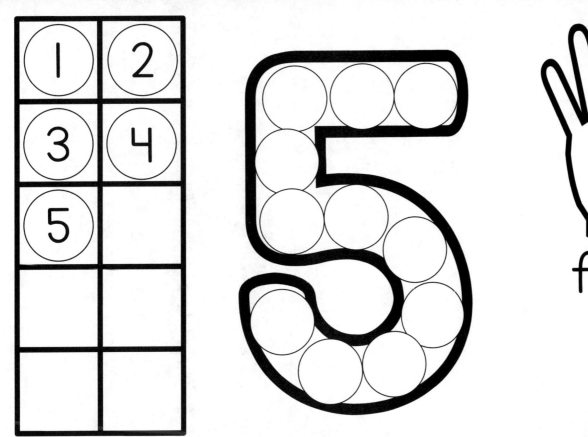

five

Dot the dots to get to 5.

①② + ④⑤ = 5
③

① ② + ⑤ = 5
③ ④

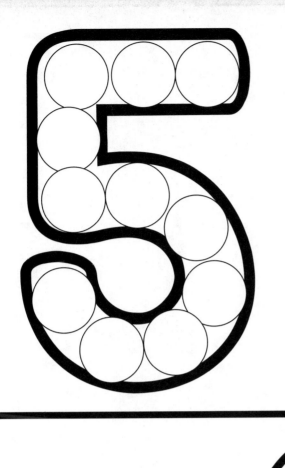

Count and dot the five flower petals.

five

Find and dot all the number 5's.

5	1	0	7	5
6	0	5	4	1
2	0	5	3	6
9	5	1	2	4
8	5	0	8	0

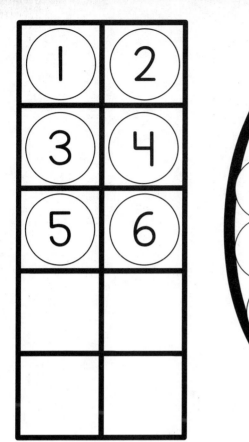

six

Dot the dots to get to 6.

(1) (2)
(3) (4) **+** (5) (6) **=** 6
___

(1) (2)
(3) **+** (4) (5)
(6) **=** 6
___

6

6

Count and dot the
six butterflies.

six **6**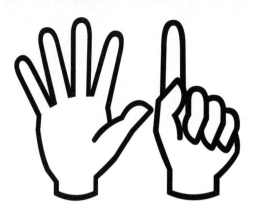

Find and dot all the number 6's.

0	6	3	0	7
2	2	6	4	5
6	7	5	3	6
9	2	6	2	1
0	1	0	6	8

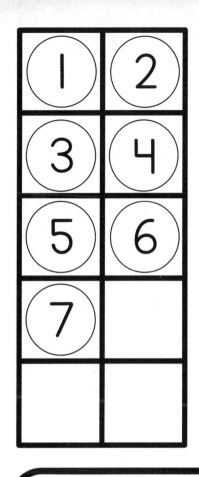

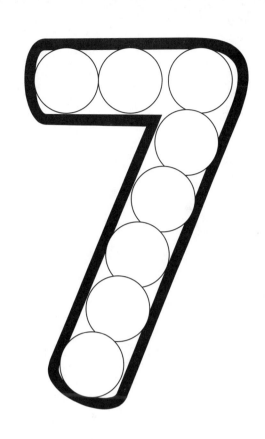

seven

Dot the dots to get to 7.

(1) (2) (3)
(4) (5) **+** (6) (7) **=** 7
___

(1) (2)
(3) (4) **+** (5) (6)
(7) **=** 7
___

Count and dot
the seven mice.

seven 7

Find and dot all the number 7's.

7	4	1	0	3
0	7	6	2	7
6	4	5	0	7
8	0	2	9	1
7	3	4	7	9

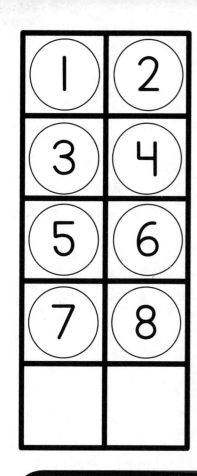

eight

Dot the dots to get to 8.

(1) (2) (3)
(4) (5) (6)   +   (7) (8)   =   8 ____

(1) (2)   (5) (6)
(3) (4)   +   (7) (8)   =   8 ____

_____

Count and dot
the eight stars.

eight 8

Find and dot all the number 8's.

2	8	4	1	0
0	3	8	2	5
8	7	1	4	7
2	0	8	9	6
8	2	3	0	8

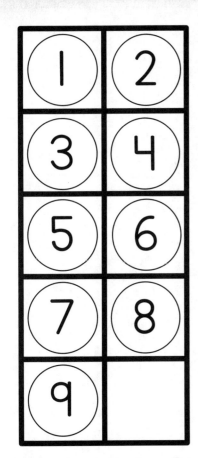

nine

Dot the dots to get to 9.

(1) (2) (3)
(4) (5) (6)   **+**   (7) (8)
(9)   **=** 9
___

(1) (2) (3)
(4) (5)   **+**   (6) (7)
(8) (9)   **=** 9
___

___

Count and dot the nine ladybugs.

nine q

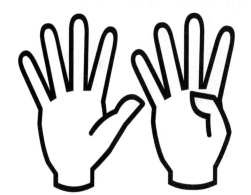

Find and dot all the number 9's.

3	7	6	2	1
0	9	9	8	0
5	9	1	7	9
4	0	3	9	5
2	9	2	0	5

1	2
3	4
5	6
7	8
9	10

10

ten

Dot the dots to count to 10.

1 2 3
4 5 6
+
7 8
9 10
= 10

1 2 3
4 5
6 7
+
8 9
10
= 10

Count and dot
the ten bubbles.

ten 10

Find and dot all the number 10's.

6	10	8	2	1
4	7	3	10	0
5	4	10	7	1
10	0	3	2	10
2	10	6	0	5

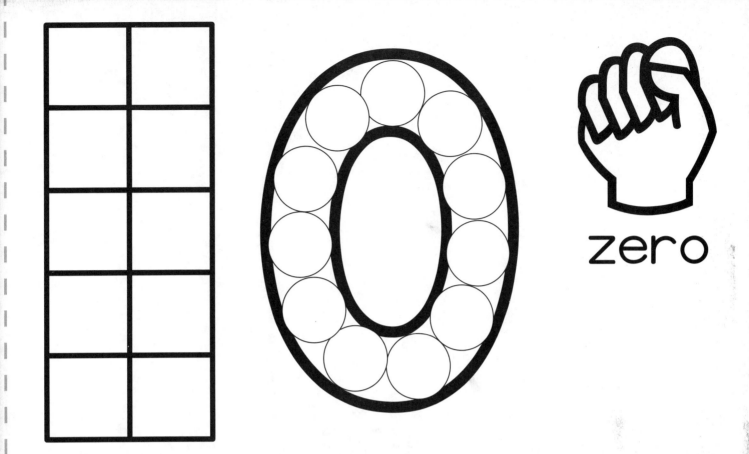

zero

Dot the dots to get to 0.

0 + 0 = 0

0 + 0 = 0

Hint: This box should have no dots!

Dot the word zero.

zero

Find and dot all the number 0's.

(2) (0) (4) (3) (0)

(0) (1) (3) (0) (1)

(7) (0) (0) (5) (0)

(0) (5) (9) (0) (6)

(8) (7) (0) (9) (0)